IF I
PLUG
MY
EARS,
GOD
CAN'T
TELL
ME
WHAT
TO
DO

IF I PLUG MY EARS, GOD CAN'T TELL ME WHAT TO DO

& OTHER WAYS WE MISS OUT ON GOD'S ADVENTURES

JESSIE CLEMENCE

 Discovery House.

If I Plug My Ears, God Can't Tell Me What to Do:
And Other Ways We Miss Out on God's Adventures

Discovery House is affiliated with Our Daily Bread Ministries,
Grand Rapids, Michigan.

Requests for permission to quote from this book should be directed to:
Permissions Department, Discovery House, P.O. Box 3566, Grand Rapids,
MI 49501, or contact us by email at permissionsdept@dhp.org.

Interior design by Sherri L. Hoffman

Library of Congress Cataloging-in-Publication Data
Clemence, Jessie.
    If I plug my ears, God can't tell me what to do : and other ways we
    miss out on God's adventures / Jessie Clemence.
        pages   cm
    Includes bibliographical references.
    ISBN 978-1-62707-190-1
    1. Obedience—Religious aspects—Christianity. 2. Listening—
    Religious aspects—Christianity. I. Title.
    BV4647.O2C54 2015
    248.4—dc23   015003382

Printed in the United States of America

First printing in 2015

Contents

CHAPTER 1

Playing Hide-and-Seek

ISAIAH 55:10–11

As the rain and the snow come down from heaven, and do not return to it without watering the earth and making it bud and flourish, so that it yields seed for the sower and bread for the eater, so is my word that goes out from my mouth: It will not return to me empty, but will accomplish what I desire and achieve the purpose for which I sent it.

Picture this. The year: 1985. The location: a farmhouse in southwest Michigan. The scene: it's dark, just before bedtime. My father is playing hide-and-seek with my brother, my sister, and me. Our mother is enjoying twenty minutes of peace with her sewing machine while we play with Dad. Suddenly, you hear screaming as my father jumps out of a dark closet and yells, "BOO!" to his three terrified children.

As soon as the terror subsides, we beg him to do it again.

Welcome to hide-and-seek, Morgan style. When these memories roll through my mind, I can still feel my stomach flip-flopping as the adrenaline rushes through my nine-year-old body. I can still feel my brother falling to the ground as I knock him out of the way in my fright. And I still barely notice my baby sister at all as I trample her four-year-old body. I don't have any excuse—I'm just scared. Down the hallway I thump through the darkness to the light at my mother's sewing table.

Those evenings of hide-and-seek are also some of my best memories from childhood. Who doesn't love to see Daddy stuffed in a closet, hiding between his Carhartt coveralls and three pairs of snow pants? Who doesn't love to be a little scared every once in a while—under extremely controlled conditions? I know I did.

But now I'm all grown up, so I don't need to play hide-and-seek anymore. If I want to spend time with my dad, I break something around my house and then beg him to come over and fix it. Or I develop a pressing need for an omelet from Cracker Barrel and suggest he join me there. Dad certainly doesn't need to ball himself up behind the recliner in a darkened living room to make me happy now.

If I've learned how to spend time with my earthly father, why do I keep trying to play hide-and-seek with my heavenly Father? Why am I always hiding in plain view when He calls? Why do I tend to cover my eyes and plug my ears, assuming that if I can't see or hear Him, He can't see me?

Because that's pretty ridiculous. I'm pretty sure God can see me there, with my feet pulled up under me, hunched into a big ball of *I'm-Ignoring-You* on the couch we've had for fifteen years. He knows where to find me; that's my spot.

Yet the scene repeats itself through the years. God speaks to me; I plug my ears and pretend not to hear. God calls to me; I make believe I'm busy with super-important other things. Because, you know, Lord, that kitchen floor is not going to mop itself. And the children are not yet old enough to drive themselves to hockey practice.*

Am I alone here? Am I the only one who has problems hearing and obeying God? I'm going to guess I'm *not* alone, that perhaps you also have trouble hearing God when He calls and then following through with your end of the bargain. Because we're all human, and that's what humans do. History has proven this, from Adam and Eve to Moses to Peter to the modern-day church.

* Just kidding. My kids don't play hockey. I can bet dollars to donuts they're downstairs right now, reading books or writing plays or playing video games. Sports make us nervous.

What Is God Asking You to Do?

What God requests of each person is as varied as people themselves. Here, let's make a little list, just to clarify what we're talking about. These are real-life examples from the lives of some of my friends, revealing what they felt God was asking them to do:

▶ Sell the house and move to Texas for a new job.

▶ Move to Alaska to be a missionary.

▶ Homeschool the kids.

▶ Take care of aging parents.

▶ Go back to college.

▶ Quit a good job to stay home with the kids.

▶ Stick to a budget to begin tithing.

▶ Become foster parents.

▶ Adopt children internationally.

▶ Work overtime to support a spouse whose ministry makes no income.

These are just a few modern-day examples. We haven't even touched on the biblical ones:

Remember Moses? He heard from God through a burning bush and ended up leading God's people in the desert for forty years.

Remember David? He was anointed as the next king but then had to wait many years before he was crowned.

Remember Peter? Despite denying Jesus loudly and clearly, Jesus used him mightily in the beginning years of the church. Each of these started with God asking His child to trust Him and obey—then to follow through. And every example has the same outcome. God orchestrated every detail to accomplish His will.

Notice the pattern? From my friend Betsy, who moved to Dallas, to the apostle John, who wrote the book of Revelation from the island of Patmos two thousand years ago, God needed only a heart willing to say yes. When we whisper "yes" to our heavenly Father, He responds, "Great! I'll make all the arrangements!" And we are off on the adventure of a lifetime.

))) **When we whisper "yes" to our heavenly Father, He responds, "Great! I'll make all the arrangements!" And we are off on the adventure of a lifetime.**

Some people are going to get the *big calls*. You know what I mean—those people called to Africa to run orphanages or those who hear God asking them to leave jobs with large salaries to start a ministry with no salary at all. Many of us know people who get these big calls, but we're confident that we aren't called to them ourselves. Does that mean we don't need to pay attention to the rest of this book? Are we safe to continue doing whatever we want?

No! It's impossible for every Christian to start an orphanage, move to Africa as a missionary, *and* also start a local homeless shelter. We all can't do it all. But this shouldn't stop us from seeking to do exactly what God has for us to do. He might ask us to be the person who makes a good income and then financially supports the missionary. He might ask us to stay in our own neighborhood and reach out to the neighbors who haven't been to church since 1995. He might start by asking us to soften our hearts and allow Him access to the deepest part of who we are so He can work miracles in places no one else may ever see.

No follower of Christ can wisely pretend that God doesn't have a plan for his or her life. The truth is that He has a plan for each of us—just as He had a plan for the Jews who were in captivity in sixth-century BC Babylon. In Jeremiah 29:11 we read that God told them: "For I know the plans I have for you . . ." which makes it pretty clear. Likewise, God is involved in our lives today, and He even has a plan. (See Ephesians 1:11.) In our own estimation we may seem small and somewhat insignificant, but it's not our perception that's important here. We need to be looking for God's perspective, because He didn't create His plan from our frame of reference—He used His own! And it's big! And exciting! Then He even planned our little lives to fit into His big, exciting plan. Once we realize He has a purpose for us, it's a little easier to understand why He would call us to something we can't possibly understand.

)))   **Sometimes God calls us to new things that radically change our lives. Sometimes God calls us to new things that radically change our hearts.**

Sometimes God calls us to new things that radically change our lives. Sometimes God calls us to new things that radically change our hearts. A year from now some of us will be in places we never expected. We might be living in a new country, with new children, and with a new career. But some of us are going to listen to God and—from the outside—not one little thing will change. We'll still be in the same house, with the same people, driving the same old Buick. But our hearts might be brand-new, which means our lives will be brand-new even when nothing physically changes.

Here's a perfect example of what I mean. Jesus gave His disciples the Great Commission and told them to go and reach other people for Him. He told them to make sure those new followers were baptized and taught to follow His commands (Matthew 28:19–20). So that covers the big calls. Going and reaching and baptizing and teaching—big stuff. But what are those commands we need to teach? He said: "'Love the Lord your God with all your heart and with all your soul and with all your mind.' This is the first and greatest commandment. And the second is like it: 'Love your neighbor as yourself.' All the Law and the Prophets hang on these two commandments" (Matthew 22:37–40).

Jesus was talking to all of us. As followers of Christ, each of us is called to love God with all our hearts, to love the people He's given us, and to teach others about Christ. That covers everyone, whether we have the big call to be a missionary or the more familiar call to parent our children well. Whether we're twenty-one years old or sixty-one. Whether we've been a Christian for twenty years or twenty minutes.

Once we understand that those foundational principles apply to everyone, things get interesting. Each follower of Christ is given a different set of talents, a different set of circumstances, and a different amount of time to live out those basic commands. There is no one-size-fits all approach to loving God and loving others. Yes, some of us are going to get the *big calls*. Our lives are about to become very different from anything we have considered before. But none of us is called to live a stagnant life; we are each called to an active faith. Whether we're about to adopt three children from China or volunteer at the local elementary school, our task is to work out God's basic commands within the specifics of our own lives. The commands and the Great Commission may be simple, but that doesn't make them *easy*. As we move forward, we will discuss the many issues that may come up as we work out God's call in our own lives.

We're going to stop plugging our ears and hoping God stops talking to us. When He calls, we will answer. No more missing out on the adventures He has planned for us.

Moses and That Burning Bush

Let's start in the book of Exodus, chapters 3 and 4. You'll see that our friend Moses was wandering around, watching the sheep for his father-in-law. He was near the mountain of God, which was possibly the only excitement he had for the day. (Oooh, a big hill. Whoopee!) Imagine being a shepherd. You have no iPod, no smartphone.* It's just you and hundreds of sheep. In the sun. Day after day after day. The sheep eat; you watch them. The sheep need a new pasture, and you lead them, half awake. Ferocious sheep-eating beasts attack, and you beat them off with a stick. At least you're now awake.

I don't intend to demean the career of shepherding. It's a valuable position in many communities, even today. But other than the shepherds at Christ's birth, we don't usually think of them making significant contributions to the events of history. You don't really remember Moses the Shepherd, do you? And why not? Because God had other plans for his life, and they were *huge*.

Exodus 2 tells us that Moses had started life quite . . . shall we say . . . interestingly. His parents had hidden him by a river in the reeds, the Pharaoh's daughter adopted him, and he was raised in the palace. Moses spent his formative years in wealth and privilege. He was likely well educated, greatly entertained, and gainfully employed. As an adult, he killed an Egyptian who was beating a fellow Hebrew. After he fled for his life to Midian, his career path consisted of herding sheep, watching sheep, and hiding in the desert while he kept the sheep safe. Most likely, his days were endlessly the same. Perhaps God moved Moses from being a prince to a shepherd to teach him how boring life can be when we aren't fulfilling our intended purpose.

So, back to Exodus 3: Moses and the sheep were moseying around, and all of a sudden he saw a bush burning. This was a welcome break from the routine, so he hurried right over to the excitement. He was expecting blazing shrubbery, but he got

* What Moses would have Tweeted: "In the wilderness with sheep again today. Feels like yesterday."

more than that. He heard the Almighty make contact with him. God had seen the misery of the Israelites, and He was about to do something about it. Moses, of course, was His chosen vessel to end the Israelites' suffering in Egypt.

Apparently, Moses had long before given up any dreams of being important. His life now revolved around his family, the sheep, and whatever else folks did out there in the boonies thousands of years ago. Maybe he sat around and thought about the past—about being fed grapes by babes in togas, or about enjoying the breeze created by palm fans—but he probably assumed his future was going to look exactly like his present. Hot. Boring. Normal.

But speaking from that blazing shrub, God explained His plan to Moses. It was simple: "I am sending you to Pharaoh to bring my people the Israelites out of Egypt" (Exodus 3:10). God rarely complicates our life with His details. He knows that if we have too many details we'll cling to the plan instead of to Him. Moses responded to God's announcement with a string of excuses so long it's almost funny. *"Why would Pharaoh listen to me? What do I tell them your name is? What if they don't believe me? Have you noticed I don't speak very well? And also, **could you send someone else**?"* I can feel the desperation in the poor man's voice, can't you? The guy started out the day tending sheep, and this was not how he expected—or wanted—it to end.

God had a response for every excuse, every practical concern Moses had. He replied, in effect: "I will be with you. My name is I AM WHO I AM. Here, I have some miracles planned. They should get Pharaoh's attention. I know you're worried about your ability to speak, but I created your mouth. I will help you! Still not convinced? Fine, your brother Aaron is on the way. **Now take your staff and GO!**"* (see Exodus 3:12, 14; 4:2–17).

---

* Next Tweet from Moses: "Note to self: skip excuses next time. Interaction with bush will go better."

I love Exodus 4:14: "Then the LORD's anger burned against Moses and he said . . ." Don't you love it when someone *else* irritates the Lord? It gives me hope that perhaps I am not the only blockhead on earth. The almighty God was there in front of Moses in a burning bush. Even with this amazing display and direct contact with God, Moses still hesitated. He must have been very scared, or very stubborn. But isn't it encouraging that God loved Moses enough to use him, even though he was so terrified and mulish?

Fast-forward thousands of years. Where are the Israelites now? All over the earth! They aren't in Egypt, still slaving away and making bricks. Where is the Pharaoh? Not in charge any longer. This proves a point—when God needs something done, it is going to get done. If He's going to use a human to do it, it's still going to get done, even when that human is, um, human. We are weak. We make huge mistakes. We sin so grievously that we break God's heart. Even on our best days, with our best intentions, we are small, ineffective, and immature.

This does not matter to God. In fact, it is precisely what He is looking for. Our weakness points out His strength. Our limits bring glory to His omnipotence. First Corinthians 1:26–29 says:

> Remember, dear brothers and sisters, that few of you were wise in the world's eyes or powerful or wealthy when God called you. Instead, God chose things the world considers foolish in order to shame those who think they are wise. And he chose things that are powerless to shame those who are powerful. God chose things despised by the world, things counted as nothing at all, and used them to bring to nothing what the world considers important. As a result, no one can ever boast in the presence of God. (NLT)

By ourselves, we are nothing. We can't do anything. We know this, and I think this is why we plug our ears when He comes calling our name. What can we possibly do to help *God*? But when God orchestrates and arranges our lives, there are no limits. He knows no bounds, and whatever He has planned, He will do. Why would we hide from God when He's capable of handling every challenge we face?

What is God asking you to do? Do your excuses make you sound like Moses? Perhaps you don't feel educated enough, rich enough, or old enough. Maybe you think no one would listen to you or that your past is too dark for God to use you. You could be worrying about disappointing your parents or throwing away your plans for the future. Even when we want to obey God, there can be actual real-life problems standing in our way. Those "problems" are another reason we plug our ears when God calls. Let's face it; Moses might not have wandered over to that bush if he had known what God was about to ask him to do.

Moses knew he was a murderer.

Moses knew he was not welcome among his own people.

Moses knew he was really good with a flock of sheep and really bad with a flock of people. None of those problems screams out, "Excellent Leadership Qualities!"

Lest you think I'm picking on poor Moses, let me tell you a little story about myself. A few years (yes, years) ago, God said to me, "Write a book."

I plugged my ears.

But He started up again, a little louder each time. I finally couldn't ignore Him anymore; the idea of writing a book was always at the back of my mind. I sat down with the laptop, wrote out an outline, and started my book. My favorite genre is "cozy mysteries." You know, someone gets shot or poisoned, the quirky detective shows up, and the genius solves the mystery against all odds. (Think Agatha Christie.) I've read about three thousand of these books, so I decided to write one.

The 50 percent of a book I did write wasn't half bad. I just couldn't come up with any more words or plot. So I said, "There, God. I did it. I failed. But at least I tried, so that's out of the way. Now what do you have next?"

God said, "Write a book."

I said, "I tried that, remember?"

He said, "Write a book."

Friends would make offhand comments like, "When are you writing that book?" They didn't even know I *had* written a book—or at least half of one. So I sat back down and started a new mystery. I wrote seven pages, twice. I hated every page, and I deleted it all. Twice. Finally—convinced that I was hearing the voices in my head again, not the Almighty—I gave up and started thinking about new career paths.

Somewhere in the middle of dusting my living room, God whispered to me a few weeks later, "Maybe it's not supposed to be fiction." Well, wow! I hadn't thought of that. My mind started whirling, and I began to think of all the great nonfiction writing that had made an impact on my life.

I sat down, started a new outline, wrote four chapters of a new book, and then deleted it all. It just wasn't working. So again, I said, "There. Tried again, failed again. I really am hearing voices, and *I am done*. Seriously, what do you want me to do?" I had just read a devotional on listening to God, and I put Him to the test. For two weeks I tried to listen to God. I sat quietly (not my strong suit), I opened up my heart, and I shut my mouth. I listened.

And God said to me, "Write a book."

I am dense and stubborn, but I am not an idiot. So here we are, in the first chapter of my book. I tell you all of this so you know that God is asking me to do big things too, and I am totally out of my comfort zone. I have a bachelor's degree in family studies from Western Michigan University. It's a great school and I loved my major, but it isn't exactly a degree in literature from Harvard or a master's in practical theology from Indiana Wesleyan University. I just know that God has given me a task, I am not skilled enough to accomplish it, and He's going to get it done anyway. I want His words to be on these pages, so I am listening and praying and studying His Word.

I pray that your heart will be open as you continue to read, not because I have such fascinating insights into the Word of God, but because He has something for you here, and you need to absorb it. We are going to study our weaknesses in light of God's plan for our lives. We may be a mess, but this isn't going to stop God.

Please meditate on the following passage found in Isaiah 55:8–13. It contains principles that are foundational to understanding obedience and God's plan for our lives.

> "For my thoughts are not your thoughts, neither are your ways my ways," declares the LORD. "As the heavens are higher than the earth, so are my ways higher than your ways and my thoughts than your thoughts.
>
> "As the rain and the snow come down from heaven, and do not return to it without watering the earth and making it bud and flourish, so that it yields seed for the sower and bread for the eater, so is my word that goes out from my mouth:
>
> "It will not return to me empty, but will accomplish what I desire and achieve the purpose for which I sent it.
>
> "You will go out in joy and be led forth in peace; the mountains and hills will burst into song before

you, and all the trees of the field will clap their hands. Instead of the thornbush will grow the juniper, and instead of briers the myrtle will grow.

"This will be for the LORD'S renown, for an everlasting sign, that will endure forever."

God's ways are higher than our ways, and His plan is greater than anything we could imagine. Are we willing to move with Him to that next step? Are we willing to unplug our ears and climb off our spot on the couch? Are we ready to stop hiding from our Father? I hope we are, because God wants to take us each on an adventure. Here we go!

QUESTIONS TO HELP YOU EVALUATE YOUR NEXT STEP WITH GOD:

1. What is God asking *you* to do? Does it involve a huge life change, a huge heart change, or both?

2. On a scale of 1 to 10, how do you feel about God's plan? (1 means your fingers are still jammed in your ears; 10 means you are enthusiastically in the middle of the scariest project of your life.)

3. If you step out in faith and obey God, what changes do you anticipate? Are you prepared for them?

4. What reasons do you have for not following God in this particular request?

5. What will God have to provide for you to accomplish this task?

6. Rewrite Isaiah 55:8–9 in your own words.

7. Look up the following passages of Scripture and apply them to your current situation:
   a. Esther 4:12–14
   b. Matthew 8:23–27
   c. Luke 5:1–11

Betsy and Her Family Move to Texas

Betsy and her husband, Matt, grew up in southwest Michigan. I don't know if two people could be more connected to their community. Their extended families lived within a few miles, their kids attended the same Christian school Betsy and Matt had attended, and they worshiped in the same church with their grandparents and cousins. I don't think there's a place in Kalamazoo where they couldn't find someone they knew. Betsy had a thriving clientele for her hair salon, my own luscious locks included.

As you can imagine, this is a nice, cozy, snug way to live. But Matt started thinking about finding a new job, one that would meet the family's needs better and provide a more positive work environment. What started as an idle thought turned out to be God, sparking a move to Texas—1,060 miles from Kalamazoo. This is what Betsy said about the move:

I don't think I've ever spent so much time in prayer. I felt that God was directly speaking to Matt and me through answered prayers, but I continued to pray, pray, and pray. I wanted to seek God's will and not my own. God opened doors and smoothed the way to show us what we needed to do. He gave us our own human will to decide whether or not we wanted to walk through those doors and follow Him, but it was very clear that He was providing a job for Matt in Texas.

It is hard to obey God; it is much easier just to ignore His calling and stay in our comfortable bubble. I wanted to obey Him, though, because He has our best interests at heart and would lead us through this.

The Sunday after we decided to move, God spoke to us through our pastor. The sermon was about leaving your comfortable life behind and going where God is leading. It was a powerful sign of confirmation. I was both scared and excited! I was excited to know

God's plan for us, but I was scared about how it would all work out. I feel that my fear pushed me closer to God to lean on Him.

We've had to make a lot of sacrifices to follow God's call. We left family, friends, school, and church. It was very hard leaving all that behind and seeing how we were not only affecting our kids' lives but also all of those close to us. I have a new appreciation for family, friends, and the community we belonged to. This move has made me realize that it is very easy to take things for granted.

We've had to make some sacrifices, but my spiritual life has grown by leaps and bounds. It has made us grow closer as a family, and we've really gotten to know our kids. I realized that God always provides! My eyes have been opened to truly listening and seeking God's will. When we take away the limitations we put on God, it is amazing what He can do in our lives.

Giving God complete control of our lives and our kids' lives has been really hard. I like to be in control. I like to be organized and have everything planned out. It's hard to follow His will when I may not totally believe it's what is best for our family. In my eyes what was best was to stay in a "comfortable life," surrounded by friends and family.

Here's the problem with doing that: It doesn't draw us closer to our Lord. It makes us lazy and self-sufficient. God has taught me to let go and give Him control, and He will provide. As much as I love my kids, God loves them a thousand times more and knows what is best for them. That has been something I remind myself of daily!

If I had to do it over, I wouldn't change anything. We don't know where God is leading us next, so we must have faith and see where we will end up. It is all according to His plan and purpose. He is teaching us valuable life lessons here that we would never have realized if we had stayed in Michigan.

I do know this: If you pray for God to use you and take control of your life, prepare yourself for an amazing, life-changing experience. God knows the big picture, and that is where we have to believe that someday His purpose for us will be revealed. If you pray for God to open doors, don't be afraid to walk through them. You never know where He is leading you! ■

CHAPTER 2

Battling the Sinful Nature

1 TIMOTHY 1:15–16

This is a trustworthy saying, and everyone should accept it: "Christ Jesus came into the world to save sinners"—and I am the worst of them all. But God had mercy on me so that Christ Jesus could use me as a prime example of his great patience with even the worst sinners. Then others will realize that they, too, can believe in him and receive eternal life. (NLT)

If there's one thing that can hinder the accomplishment of God's plan for our lives, it's our ugly, dark, sinful natures. The temptations we face are as diverse as the people on earth. Some of us lie; others steal. Some of us can't kick sexual addictions or the craving for material possessions. Some of us are lazy; others are self-righteous.

It doesn't matter what your issue is. God knows. He knows what you have done in the past, He knows what you want to do right now, and He knows where you're going to end up in the future. And although there is no life that cannot be redeemed by Christ's atoning blood, sins of the past can have a horrible hold on a Christian. Some mistakes are so huge that it seems as though we are doomed to never reach our full potential. And in fact, if we are holding on to those sins and pretending that they don't affect our relationship with God, they *can* keep us from reaching our full potential. However, once we understand that we have sinned and then ask God for forgiveness, we are once again in full relationship with our loving Father. There is no sin too huge for God to forgive.

))) We are made right with God by placing our faith in Jesus Christ. And this is true for everyone who believes, no matter who we are. For everyone has sinned; we all fall short of God's glorious standard. Yet God freely and graciously declares that we are righteous. He did this through Christ Jesus when he freed us from the penalty for our sins (Romans 3:22–25 NLT).

You may be whispering to yourself, "But you don't know what I've done. God could never use me." And in love, I must tell you you're wrong.

Let's talk about one of my all-time favorite sinners, King David. In 2 Samuel 11 the guy checked off all the major sins in one story—beginning with the seduction of the beautiful Bathsheba. The Israelite army was marching around the countryside, killing off enemies and securing their land. David was still in Jerusalem for whatever reason, and he was walking around on his rooftop. The lovely Bathsheba was taking a bath where he could see her and it appears that he stood and took a nice, long look. He even sent someone to find out about her which is when he learned that this beautiful bather was married to a man named Uriah. (Sins No. 1 & No. 2: lust and covetousness.) He sent for her and then slept with her. (Sin No. 3: adultery.) Now, I'm no expert on ancient Jewish kings, but I'm pretty sure David wasn't hurting for sex. The guy already had a few wives, possibly even a whole harem. So what on earth made the man send for a woman he knew was married? Two reasons come to mind: He was a man, and he was a king, which made him a man who was used to getting what he wanted. (Sin No. 4: general pigheadedness.)

Bathsheba got pregnant, and so now our friend David had a real predicament on his hands. Everyone knew that Bathsheba's husband, Uriah, was out battling on David's behalf, not at home sleeping with his pretty wife. So David called Uriah in from battle, hoping that while he was home he would have some romantic time with Bathsheba. Everyone would think the baby was Uriah's, and the problem would have ended. (Sin No. 5: deception.) But poor Uriah actually had some integrity, and he just slept on the ground, along with the king's servants. Since David's problem was not going away politely, he got aggressive and had Uriah put on the front lines, where he was sure to be killed. (Sin No. 6: murder.)

So there we have it, folks. Unless you have been running around having random sex with strangers and then killing off their spouses, you have not yet hit David's all-time low. This man was one of God's favorites, even after this whole mess. Is this absorbing into your brain? It does not matter what you have done. God is not done with you yet.

But wait a minute! What if the story ended right there for David? What if he just walked away from this colossal disaster and pretended it never happened? He could have. He was the king, and if he decided to ignore the poor pregnant woman and their unborn child, who was going to stop him? I think this is the key to why God loved David so much—David's heart was tender. He was not callous to his pregnant lover. He did not abandon this child. He brought Bathsheba into his household and married her. Granted, he had not yet repented, and it took a prophet from the Lord to get him to that point. But when the prophet Nathan came to David and pointed out what he had stolen, David repented. He could have had the prophet killed, but David knew the truth. His heart was tender toward the Lord.

Our repentance is the only thing God needs to take our sin and wash it away. First John 1:9 reminds us that "if we confess our sins, he is faithful and just and will forgive us our sins and purify us from all unrighteousness." Christ died for nothing if we think our sin is too great for God to erase. Christ died for every sin ever committed, and that means your sin too. If you've repented but still feel that God is done with you, read on with me. What happened next to David?

It's sad, but Bathsheba's baby died. The ugly truth is that every sin has a consequence. The Bible records that David fasted and slept on the floor for seven days before the baby died, begging for God to spare his son's life. His pleading was not enough. When he learned that the child was gone, David got up, washed, and ate. He knew that he would one day go to his son, but his son would not come back to him.

Is it possible that the consequences of our sin feel as dark as David's grief? For seven days he stopped running the kingdom. His elders couldn't get him off the floor. He didn't even try to bluff to save his public image. He just cried on the floor, hungry and dirty, begging for God to listen. When the baby died on the seventh day, he could have just stayed there for a while longer. He could have taken himself out to the battle in hopes that he also would have been killed. He didn't. David did not give up. He went to his wife and comforted her.

Also, he got her pregnant again. Men!

Do you know who was born this time? The baby's name was Solomon! King Solomon! After sincere repentance, God brings restoration. David wrote Psalm 51 after this incident with Bathsheba. The psalm says this in verses 7–12:

> Cleanse me with hyssop, and I will be clean; wash me,
> and I will be whiter than snow. Let me hear joy and

gladness; let the bones you have crushed rejoice. Hide your face from my sins and blot out all my iniquity. Create in me a pure heart, O God, and renew a stead-fast spirit within me. Do not cast me from your presence or take your Holy Spirit from me. Restore to me the joy of your salvation and grant me a willing spirit, to sustain me.

David's words are a testament to God's unending mercy with us. So let us not give up. We have sinned, but it may be that God will take our repentance and turn it into something beautiful that will honor His name. I firmly believe that the only thing God needs from us is a tender, willing heart. If we fail, He is not surprised. His plans for our lives will succeed regardless of our mistakes.

A Lifestyle of Sin

This is not to say, of course, that we can continue in our sin and assume that God is going to be fine with it because of His merciful nature. There are sixty-six books in the Bible, and all of them are pretty clear on what God thinks about sin. To be sure, I am talking about when we are living in a sinful lifestyle on purpose. I'm not talking about the time we shout a swear word when we break our big toe on the china cabinet. I'm talking about when we know something is wrong, we do it anyway, and then we do it again, again, again . . .

I think we all know people who chose to live in sin until it exploded in their face. Perhaps a friendship grew into an affair that destroyed two families. Or a few stolen items here and there turned into a five-year stint in jail. A few drinks after work turned into steady drinking alone, then a life controlled by alcohol. Everyone knows an example.

Often the pain is felt most keenly by people who have no control over the situation: The children in the broken family, the spouse left alone to support the family, or the mother who visits the jail. Our choices never affect only ourselves. The consequences ripple outward—even to generations after us.

What if you *are* the example everyone thinks about? What if your life is so full of sin that it is referred to as a lifestyle? It doesn't have to be a two-year illicit affair. It could be gossiping, gluttony, lying—you name it. Leave it now. Walk away, because God loves you too much to let this sin continue in your life. He will allow the consequences, and they will not be pleasant. God is waiting for you. You can have peace. You can make new choices and live a different life. God will give you the wisdom and the strength if you ask.

What if at one time you *were* the example? What if you were a modern version of King David? Some sins are so big that they define who we are or who we used to be. Even after the repentance and the life changes, they hang in the past and wave their red memory flags at us.

This is a hard suggestion that I'm about to make, so don't pass out on me. Maybe that thing you are desperate to erase from your history is the very thing God is about to ask you to use. The most effective ministries often start with one person who is willing to take his or her experience and turn it around to help others. Maybe you were a promiscuous teenager. There are still teens out there who are thinking about having sex. Maybe you stole someone's husband or embezzled somebody's money. Someone out there needs to know what you learned, what God's forgiveness feels like, and how to make a new life. Don't be afraid to give this area to God and grow from your experience.

There is no mistake too horrible for God to redeem. In fact, Ephesians 2:4–10 says this:

> But because of his great love for us, God, who is rich
> in mercy, made us alive with Christ even when we
> were dead in transgressions—it is by grace you have
> been saved. And God raised us up with Christ and
> seated us with him in the heavenly realms in Christ
> Jesus, in order that in the coming ages he might show
> the incomparable riches of his grace, expressed in his
> kindness to us in Christ Jesus. For it is by grace you
> have been saved, through faith—and this not from
> yourselves, it is the gift of God—not by works, so that
> no one can boast. For we are God's handiwork, cre-
> ated in Christ Jesus to do good works, which God
> prepared in advance for us to do.

I love that passage of Scripture because it is full of *grace*. It's
by grace—unmerited favor—we are saved. Grace makes us alive
with Christ, and grace gives us the ability to move beyond what
we *were* to what God intends for us *to be*. Let's move forward
into that grace, shall we?

Let's Define Sin Even Further

Some sin is shocking and hard to get over. We might have trans-
gressions in our lives that affect the rest of our years, and we just
studied how David had to try to recover from his sinful choices
long after the episode was over. He probably grieved his son for
the rest of his life, and I wouldn't doubt that the strained beginning to their relationship affected his marriage to Bathsheba.
When you know that a man is capable of summoning you to
his palace and then killing off your inconvenient husband, I'd
imagine you'd look at the guy funny every once in a while. The
sin was serious and it had serious consequences.

It can be easy to view as regrettable that drastic sort of sin, but it may seem somehow different from what is going on in our own little lives. But when we boil down each sinful choice to its essence, *the root of every sin is the same.* Big sins, little sins, medium sins—each of them starts with a person choosing his own way over God's way. If we go back to the first sin in the garden of Eden, we see that both Adam and Eve sinned when they ate the fruit from the Tree of the Knowledge of Good and Evil. Is eating fruit a sin? No, not unless God specifically told you not to eat the fruit and you did it anyway. The sin for our first parents was choosing their way over God's way.

Anytime we choose ourselves over God, we're sinning. If we have clear directions from the Word of God and we ignore them, we're sinning. God gave us firm guidelines about everything—what we think in our hearts, what we say, how we love people, and the choices we make. So we can't simply look at adultery and murder and assume that we're safe because we haven't done *that* yet. If we take a quick peek at Jesus' words in Matthew 5:21–30, we're reminded that He set the standards pretty high—"anyone who says 'You fool!' will be in danger of the fire of hell" and "anyone who looks at a woman lustfully has already committed adultery with her in his heart." He was clear; sin is an issue of the heart. Sin is not just the actions that flow from the heart.

Those sins of the heart can be even more devastating because they can build walls between us and God before we realize what is going on. The big consequences of big sins are hard to ignore, but the quieter sins we can rationalize and pretend away. That doesn't make them any less of a sin. We're still choosing our own way, opinion, or perspective over God's, which will stop us from being able to follow God to wherever He is leading us.

Let me give you a personal example. Recently, I happened to read a woman's thoughts on some of my writing, and they were not favorable. I think it's safe to say that she and I were coming from different places, spiritually speaking, but her comments haunted me for several days. Now, I know that people are going to disagree with me. I've disagreed with plenty of authors, even Christian authors, in my day. I've even thrown a book or two across a room when an author has hit a nerve and gotten my dander up. So I know what it's like to clash with a writer, and I'm fine with people feeling the same way about me.

But her comments hurt because she moved from theological disagreement to what felt like criticism of my efforts to communicate what God was teaching me. I already have issues with vulnerability when I write, so it hurt for someone to take my puny efforts and criticize my every mistake. When I finally realized why her criticism hurt so much, I realized with a resounding thump that I do this to people *all the time*. I am Super Critical Woman! Mind you, I don't post my opinion about other people's efforts on a website for the world to read, but God knows my heart, and my hidden thoughts are just as bad.

I think it's totally fine to disagree with a person. I even think it's okay to evaluate the fruit in their lives to see if it is good fruit or bad fruit. Disagreement and discernment are both acceptable. But criticizing people's efforts to serve God to the best of their ability is totally not fine. Romans 14:4 says, "Who are you to condemn someone else's servants? Their own master will judge whether they stand or fall. And with the Lord's help, they will stand and receive his approval" (NLT).

Once I realized how I'd been sinning and how badly it hurt to be on the receiving end, my eyes were opened. I repented immediately. I know this is something I'm going to have to work through for many years to come. This is a basic part of my personality, and victory here is going to be won only with the Holy Spirit's constant reminding and convicting. But as far as I'm

concerned, I will never go back. I'll never again be able to rationalize my critical spirit away as "Oh, I'm just thinking logically
here, and that person is a mess."

I don't think it's a coincidence that this episode occurred
at the exact same time I was facing a serious brick wall in my
writing. It didn't matter what I wrote; it fell flat. Every effort at
blogging, Facebooking, and Tweeting was received with a dead
thump. I could feel the hollowness of my efforts; I just couldn't
understand why nothing was working. After all, God has called
me to be a writer, right? He's asked me to do this, so why wasn't
my writing being well received? I think I found the answer. My
sin was obstructing God's work in my life. He has big places to
take us and glorious things He wants to involve us in, but He
can't and won't work with children who are hiding sin in their
hearts. First John 3:9 says, "No one who is born of God will continue to sin, because God's seed remains in them; they cannot go
on sinning, because they have been born of God."

If we go back to the first chapter, we'll recall that no matter
what our calling from God may be, we're all called to love God,
to love others, and then to share Christ with the world. Our sin
will keep us from doing that, no matter what kind of sin it may
be. All sin creates a block in our relationship with God, and we
need to be conscious of it. Working with God means doing it His
way. We can't nurture a little sin or hide a really big one and hope
God just ignores it. He won't, because He can't.

Remembering the Good News

Now that we're all stressing out about every sin we've ever committed and every future sin we might commit, let's go back to
the point. It's not about our righteousness. We can never be
good enough to win favor with God. That's why Jesus came to
earth, lived a sinless life, and died on the cross in our place. Our

acceptance of His death, burial, and resurrection is what takes our sin away and gives us full access to the Father. Likewise, that gives the Father full access to our hearts. It's not about us; it's about Christ's sacrifice on our behalf. First John 1:7–9 says:

> But if we walk in the light, as he is in the light, we have fellowship with one another, and the blood of Jesus, his Son, purifies us from all sin. If we claim to be without sin, we deceive ourselves and the truth is not in us. If we confess our sins, he is faithful and just and will forgive us our sins and purify us from all unrighteousness.

Purified from all unrighteousness! What a beautiful gift, enabling us to move forward into God's plan for our lives! Someone shout *hallelujah*, please! We need a hallelujah right now.

Taking Care of Business before We Move Ahead

I know the topic of sin is not pleasant. Who wants to wallow in all the bad choices they've ever made? I don't think any of us do, but we have to repent of all sin before we try to serve God and follow Him to the next place He has for us. Trust me when I tell you that the journey is going to be tough—so tough that we need to be in a complete and open relationship with the Father. Any sin we ignore will keep us from that perfect relationship with God, and we don't want to attempt this without His full presence. Of course, we will fail and sin in the future, but because of Jesus' sacrifice on the cross, our sins are forgiven and we can live in harmony with God. And that harmony will allow us to move with God to the place He has for us next!

STUDY QUESTIONS

1. Tough question, but it has to be asked: Is there a problem with sin you need to deal with before God can proceed with His plan for your life? What do you need to do to put this situation behind you?

2. Is there something in your past that you cannot let go? Why do you think you let that mistake define you?

3. Is there a way you can let God redeem your past for His good? Is there someone who needs to hear your story?

4. Look up the following Scripture verses and then consider God's mercy in your own life:
   a. Hosea 14:1–5
   b. Luke 7:36–50
   c. Romans 8:1–11

> Anything and everything is possible with God if we approach him with a broken spirit. We must humble ourselves, get rid of the debris in our lives, and keep leaning on him instead of our own understanding. Your future and mine are determined by this one thing: seeking after the Lord. The blessings we receive and then pass along to others all hang on this truth: "He rewards those who earnestly seek him" (Hebrews 11:6).
>
> **Jim Cymbala,** *Fresh Wind, Fresh Fire*

CHAPTER 3

Choosing Your Attitude

GENESIS 6:22

Noah did everything just as God commanded him.

In her book *A Little Salty to Cut the Sweet*, author Sophie Hudson tells hilarious stories about her southern family. One of my favorites is about her aunt Choxie and her uncle Joe, who had been married for many decades before Joe was diagnosed with Alzheimer's. One day the family schedule veered from its normal course, and Joe was unhappy about this detour. In his mind it was Wednesday, the night he and Choxie met with friends at the country club each week, an event Joe relished. As a little inside joke, they called it "prayer meeting" night.

Well, the country club was not on the agenda. The family was vacationing together and not even in the right town. They had decided to go to the mall, and on the way there Joe asked over and over and over again about "prayer meeting," only stopping to alternate his questions with pointed comments about how they needed gas for the car. Choxie, patient and saintly Choxie, spent the drive reassuring him over and over that the gas gauge was fine and explaining the agenda over and over.

There were a lot of "over and overs" involved in that little trip to the mall.

Finally, they made it to a gas station and refilled the tank. Joe had one less thing to worry about. Sophie writes that this is how it all ended. Joe said:

"Well, it looks like you have plenty of gas!" Then: "So. Are we going to prayer meeting, Mama?"

And that, my friends, was the proverbial straw that broke the Choxie's back. She leaned forward and rested her head on the steering wheel, and when she sat up again, I could see the frustration and sadness from the previous three or four days all over her face.

"Joe," she said in a calm, measured tone. "Look at me."

Their eyes met across the leather console that ran between their seats.

"We've covered this over and over again. We are not going to prayer meeting. We are NOT going to prayer meeting. Because, Joe? Where are we?"

Joe thought long and hard about her question. And after about fifteen seconds, he gave her his best, most honest answer.

"Heck if I know!" he exclaimed, and then he puckered up like a guppy, leaned over, and kissed her on the cheek.[1]

The good Lord knows that either my husband Eric or I, one day in the future, is going to lose our mind. If you look at my family history and Eric's family history, we're doomed. The mind is a fickle beast, my friends. The question is—how are we going to handle it when the time comes? Will we manage to love each other like Choxie loves Joe? Will I be that kind and gracious with him when he asks me where we're going nine hundred times then turns into the Gas Gauge Enforcer? Or will he lovingly hide the checkbook when I insist on giving away all our money to whatever pitiful organization calls and begs us for donations?

And, heaven help us all, what if we both lose our minds at the same time? Will our children handle our senility with this loving attitude? I hope the local nursing home has a room with double occupancy, just in case the kids need to check us in together while they hide our checkbook up their sleeves.

We've talked about this before—not all of us will get the assignments that require moving around the world or starting a life-altering ministry. Many of us will be called to something that barely even appears to be a calling. It might look more like a natural progression of life. Of course a wife will care for her aging husband. Of course a parent will care for a newborn infant. And yet those caregivers will tell you straight up—*it is a calling*. It might go on inside our own living rooms, in the neighborhood where we've lived for sixty years, but it is a calling. And it requires the same attitude adjustment that even the wildest call from God might demand.

Speaking of wild calls from God, let's talk about our friend Noah. If ever there was a man given a ridiculous project, it was that poor man. The assignment seems so preposterous that many non-Christians point to it and proclaim the Bible to be a pile of fairy tales. Those of us who believe, however, realize that God does whatever He wants—however He wants to do it. God could have spared Noah's life and vaporized everyone else on the earth. He could have used fire. He could have used anything, but Genesis 6 records that He chose to use a flood, one faithful man, and a big old boat.

The Bible comments that "Noah was a righteous man, blameless among the people of his time, and he walked faithfully with God" (Genesis 6:9). Terrible evil overran the earth, which grieved God's heart. He needed to wipe the slate clean and start over. After our last chapter about sin, this truth is striking. It's more proof that sin has terrible consequences.

Out of all those people in the world—most of whom were grieving God's heart—Noah alone pleased Him. He was given the monumental job of saving the animals and his own family. His task was to build a huge boat in the middle of a field and then wait for God to start something amazing. I have no idea of how long it took the man to build that ark, but it appears to have been anywhere from eighty to a hundred years. This meant that people thought he was a nutcase for years and years. It's not like you can hide a project that large in a barn or the basement. God's plan sat right out in the open for everyone to see. Everyone had an opportunity to join Noah and be saved, but no one did except for his sons and their wives. The Bible also records that the animals all came to Noah (Genesis 7:8–9). I wonder what the neighbors thought as random animals just wandered by, called to the ark by their inbuilt homing devices.

The Bible does not record that Noah ever whined. He did not have a tantrum. He did not ignore God, plead with Him, or even pout. I don't know about you, but I am no Noah. I'm a *champion* whiner, tantrum thrower, and pouter. I'm especially good at these reactions when I think God's plan doesn't make sense. But "Noah did everything just as God commanded him" (Genesis 6:22). We gloss over this verse because it's so little, and we want to get to the exciting part of the story. You know, the part where the animals arrive and the rain starts falling and the ark starts bobbing up and down. But I want to point out that maybe this verse *is* the exciting part of the story. If it's not the most exciting, certainly it's the most important. *Noah obeyed with a good attitude.*

)))   **Common sense may scream that God's project is not reasonable, but Noah heard God's quiet voice over the bellow of common sense.**

Common sense may scream that God's project is not reasonable, but Noah heard God's quiet voice over the bellow of common sense. His obedience, coupled with a good attitude, showed tremendous maturity and faith in God, don't you think? I wish I could say the same thing about myself as I follow God's call to write, but often I can't. I'm usually held captive by common sense, which points out a full-time job would come with a regular paycheck and some benefits. I obviously haven't crossed Noah's threshold of maturity and faith.

I'm not the only one. My kids are not big fans of the challenges that come with developing maturity either. For example, when Caleb was four, I tried to teach him to button his church shirts. Caleb's wardrobe was made up almost entirely of T-shirts with cars or sports on them, but we drew the line at NASCAR on Sunday mornings. Once a week the kid had to wear a shirt with buttons to church. I started patiently, showing him how to line up the buttons with the holes, push a button through one side, and pull it through the other side. He tried, but it wasn't as easy as he had imagined. His attitude got stinky, and he started whining. I insisted that he at least try, and I even said, "Caleb, I don't expect you to do it perfectly. Just try with a good attitude." Sadly, this made him even less inclined to button the shirt. He lay down on the couch and screamed. This did not end well for the boy.

From his perspective, my request made no sense. Why should he bother with buttons when he had a drawer full of perfectly awesome T-shirts? But I had my reasons for wanting him to obey my request, and I wasn't requiring anything more than he could understand. Even if it was too much for him, I was right there and more than willing to help as long as his attitude was good. The whole experience could have ended much differently, but a bad attitude derailed everything.

How often does God ask for something and before we know it, we're in the middle of a snit? If Noah acted like we do, he would have had a tantrum before he gathered any wood! The first neighbor to point out that he was crazy would have demoralized him to the point of unraveling the whole project. But Noah "did everything just as God commanded him." God provided the instructions and the wisdom; God provided the plan of escape; and God was bigger than human common sense. We need to observe this lesson carefully, because it's very possible that God may need us to do something that seems over our heads, or too big, or just not the most common-sense way. Are we willing to do everything just as God commands us?

We've talked about the many different things God can ask us to do. Some of us have big assignments, like Noah or Moses did. God asks some people to step out in faith and to trust Him despite enormous roadblocks. When these people are faithful and choose to obey with a good attitude, God works in miraculous and mighty ways. Just think of all the movies that have been created from the story of Moses leading the Israelites out of Egypt! Think of all the nursery wallpaper designed around the story of Noah's ark! Thousands of years later we're still talking about God's faithfulness through Moses and Noah. If you've been called to something huge, let God take you there! He'll provide the wisdom, the strength, and the resources to do it! Philippians 1:6 reminds us that "he who began a good work in you will carry it on to completion until the day of Christ Jesus." We have to remember that it's really His work in the first place.

Most of us, however, are not called to do movie-worthy (or even wallpaper-worthy) things. I don't foresee anyone from Hollywood showing up to make a movie about how I parent my children or clean my bathtub. I'm not saying that such a movie wouldn't be *absolutely brilliant*, but I'm not holding my breath. Not everyone wants to sit through a real-life drama that includes me letting my kids eat too much sugar or using vinegar to scrub my bathroom fixtures. (The movie would be titled *Mediocre Mother from the Midwest*. Nice alliteration, don't you think?)

No, most of us are called to smaller things than arks and treks through the desert with a million or so of God's people. We're called to care for our aging spouses. To teach our children. To reach out to the neighbors in love. And though these choices may seem smaller and less important, they're really not. In fact, these choices are the very foundation of a Christ-centered life that reaches out to the hearts of others. We're called to be Christ's ambassadors; we're called to bring His love to the thirsty, hungry, and lonely right around us. We have to look around and see what task He's put in front of us and then do that thing with a great attitude! It doesn't matter how small it might seem to us, those little things mean big things to God. A heart that glorifies Him in the little things will glorify Him in the big things too. Matthew 25:21 says, "His master replied, 'Well done, good and faithful servant! You have been faithful with a few things; I will put you in charge of many things. Come and share your master's happiness!'" In this verse it was the faithful choices in the little things that brought the master pleasure.

My pastor, Jason Sleight, had these thoughts about this issue:

> What amazes me in Scripture is that God uses the least likely to be His instrument in a very public way. But in every case, He doesn't use those who are inactive or wasting their life. God uses people who are actively doing what they are supposed to do, even though we would not see it as significant as curing AIDS or cancer or ending hunger. Moses was actively taking care of his father-in-law's sheep. David was obeying his father by taking lunch to his brothers right before he fought Goliath. Elisha was plowing behind a couple of oxen (imagine that sight and smell every day). The disciples were doing their jobs (fishing, working for the IRS, etc.). Samuel was serving his master, Eli.

My point—everyone was doing what they were supposed to be doing or living normal lives when God called them. God never called someone who was lazy or inactive with their normal responsibilities. God wants to use us, and if we want to truly experience Him, then we must be faithful with what we are currently called to do: raise a family, work in a factory, be a secretary, go to class, pick up the trash. God gives big steps to those who are currently being faithful with the small steps.[2]

I take some comfort from Jesus' example for us. He came to earth to do something BIG. I think we'd all agree that being God in the form of man and dying on a cross and rising again is BIG. Jesus was faithful in that big set of directions from His Father. But He was also faithful in the little things. He loved the people around Him, no matter how sinful, poor, or sick. He washed dirty feet. He loved brokenhearted families. His closest friends were a handful of ragged disciples. Every step He made was with an attitude that was wholly focused on His Father's glory. Jesus said in John 15:9–12:

> "As the Father has loved me, so have I loved you. Now remain in my love. If you keep my commands, you will remain in my love, just as I have kept my Father's commands and remain in his love. I have told you this so that my joy may be in you and that your joy may be complete. My command is this: Love each other as I have loved you."

))) **"My command is this: Love each other as I have loved you" (John 15:12).**

This passage is the perfect summary of everything we're talking about. Jesus loved the Father, so He followed His commands. And what was the command? Something huge and unmanageable? No! The command was to love each other as Christ loves us. If we spend the rest of our lives following that one little command, we will not have failed the calling God has for our lives. The littlest calling is actually the biggest calling. Can you imagine what would happen to the world if every Christ-follower attempted this command every day with a good attitude? The world wouldn't know what hit it.

Whoa! Not My Strong Suit

So we've established that we need to approach every call from God with the same good attitude, right from the beginning. If we go back to Noah's assignment for a bit more discussion, I would like to point out that the Bible doesn't mention what his profession was before God spoke to him. For example, we do not know that he was a carpenter or a zookeeper. For all we know, he could have been a farmer or a baker. Perhaps a soldier or a shepherd. His skills may not have had anything to do with being an Ark Master. Or, more accurately, maybe he had never thought about being an Ark Master but had just those skills lying in the background, waiting to be used.

God may be asking you to do something, and you may be covering your ears and ignoring him—simply because it doesn't seem like something you are designed to do. Perhaps your bad attitude stems from your belief that you aren't equipped for God's request. How do you know this? You won't until you try. If your church has a bulletin notice about needing preschool teachers but you don't teach, maybe you need to get over it and try anyway. If there's a need, you may need to step outside the comfort zone and give it a whirl. What is at stake if you fail? So the preschoolers watch *VeggieTales* and eat crackers for an hour a week. No one is going to die if you aren't Super Teacher.

I know this because I have taught multiple children's classes at church. For a while I taught with my friend Michelle, and much of each Sunday involved her actually teaching the children about the Bible while I zipped around, saying, "QuentinAudrey-AbigailJASONVivianJenelleCarissa, will you please SIT DOWN and listen!" At least I was another adult body in the room when someone started throwing up. (True story.) Michelle wasn't in it alone. Sometimes she probably wished she was so I would stop reprimanding the children, but I was there whether she liked it or not. And I did my best with a decent attitude.

Philippians 2:13 reminds us that "it is God who works in you to will and to act in order to fulfill his good purpose." If God is working in us, giving us the ability to do what He is asking, how can we possibly go wrong? Our excuses sound hollow in the light of this promise.

On the Other Hand . . .

There is a balance here, of course. Just because there is a need, you might not be the one God is asking to meet it. The need might be *completely* outside your skill set, and no amount of trying with a good attitude is going to fix the problem. For example, my friend Brenda was a fantastic trustee at our church a few years ago. This means she ran the computer system that kept the finances balanced for the end-of-the-year tax statements. She handled the weekly deposit beautifully. But Brenda would have been the first person to tell you she wanted nothing to do with teaching in the children's area. She has three children she loves to pieces, and this is how she *knows* that she had no business teaching anybody else's kids. It would not have ended well for anyone if we had made her teach the three-year-olds each week.

After I graduated from Western Michigan University, I used my degree to be a social worker in the foster care system for four years. I sincerely wanted to help the families and children I met. I really did. But the stress of that job nearly killed me. I couldn't sleep at night because the responsibility was way too much. My poor dad begged me to quit. I think it was mostly because he couldn't stand hearing me whining anymore, but he was really worried. What was at stake? The very lives of the children I served. If I misread a situation or missed important information, I could have put a child in a foster or biological home where he or she could have been physically, emotionally, or sexually maimed. I quit social work when my first child, Audrey, was born, and I couldn't believe how much better life became. A willingness to serve wasn't enough in that situation. We have to be not only willing but also both equipped with skills and called to the project.

Just for fun, let's apply this idea to some of our favorite Bible characters. What if Paul had decided to go into children's ministry? His robust personality made him ideal for spreading the gospel in the early church. Persecution, prison, poverty? No problem. He was willing to take it all to complete the task God gave him. But changing diapers, reading stories to wiggly little people, and sweeping up crackers? I think he would have chosen prison any day over service in the children's department.

What about Martha, sister to Mary and Lazarus? She was the queen of hospitality, even though she focused too keenly on the housekeeping and cooking part. Jesus gently rebuked her, pointing out that she worried too much and was missing the main point (Luke 10:41–42). What if Martha had taken that rebuke to the extreme and left her house? She might have followed after Jesus and the disciples everywhere they went. The Last Supper passage might have included references to one woman who refused to do anything but sit at Jesus' feet. I'm not sure she had the skills needed to be a traveling apostle. And frankly, having a girl hanging around every single moment would have been awkward.

I will rein in my imagination now to point out that each situation we face requires us to carefully and prayerfully examine the need that exists and our ability to meet it. Is this really God's call for us? Because if it is, He'll equip us with everything we need. If it isn't, we're in for a rough ride.

Flexibility and a Willingness to Try: Key Ingredients

God gives each of us gifts, and we need to use our brains when it comes to using them. We're probably going to be able to follow through with a good attitude if our gifts are a good match for the project at hand. If you are hopeless at math and finances, He probably isn't asking you to be in charge of your church's finances. If you have a criminal record of assault with a deadly weapon, He probably isn't asking you to become a junior high teacher. It is up to us to thoughtfully and prayerfully consider what needs exist in our community and how God may be calling us to serve. Asking God for wisdom and then waiting patiently for His answer is always a good idea. Flexibility and a willingness to try never hurt either. Is God calling us to it? Then we cannot fail. Are we attempting it out of our own motivations or efforts? Then we cannot succeed.

))) **Is God calling us to it? Then we cannot fail. Are we attempting it out of our own motivations or efforts? Then we cannot succeed.**

Remember Noah and Jesus. Both men followed God's commands exactly, with a good attitude. It didn't matter if the assignment was huge or ho-hum, they were obedient in heart and actions. I pray we'll follow their good examples!

STUDY QUESTIONS

1. How's your attitude toward this project of God's? If your child had the same attitude toward a chore, would you be pleased?

2. List your three best skills.

3. List three things you know you have no business doing.

4. List three things you've never tried but might be good at (examples: painting, writing, foster parenting).

5. How do your skills, or lack thereof, factor into your attitude about this calling from God?

6. Look up the following Scriptures and then consider how our inner hearts please or displease God:

    a. Deuteronomy 11:13–15
    b. 1 Samuel 16:7
    c. Ephesians 6:5–8

You may think others have more gadgets in their utility belts than you do, you may feel like what you have in your hand is unimpressive, you may feel like this season you are in of changing diapers and driving children around town will last forever. But if God is . . . asking you to step out in obedience and use the talents and passions He's given you, then take courage and obey Him. Don't worry about what will happen after that. It's not your responsibility to achieve worldly success or to bring millions of people to Christ. You simply obey and trust God with the results.

Heather King, *Ask Me Anything, Lord*

CHAPTER 4

Listening Carefully

JOHN 10:3-5

The gatekeeper opens the gate for him, and the sheep listen to his voice. He calls his own sheep by name and leads them out. When he has brought out all his own, he goes on ahead of them, and his sheep follow him because they know his voice. But they will never follow a stranger; in fact, they will run away from him because they do not recognize a stranger's voice.

Hold on, Hoss. Let's back up this wagon train a little minute.

This book isn't going to make any sense until we discuss a key concept: *What does it mean to listen to God?* At this point in world history, God does not generally appear to us, correct? He doesn't speak audibly through burning shrubbery, the Angel of the Lord does not appear and eat dinner with us, and Jesus has not walked the earth for almost two thousand years. So if we aren't going to see Him, eat dinner with Him, or feel His nail-scarred hands, how do we think we're going to be able to listen to Him? What does that even mean?

As we've already discussed, we do have a few key items. We have the written Word. In fact, we have the Word everywhere. We have a copy on the nightstand, on the bookshelf, and maybe even on our desk at work. We have it in the New International Version, the New Living Translation, and of course the King James Version. Do you know that BibleGateway.com has over forty-five versions of the Bible available? (I just counted.) English versions! I didn't even count all the versions available in other languages. So we might not converse with the Almighty through a bush, but we certainly can crack open a copy of the Bible and start reading. That's where we start.

We've already discussed that we can hear from God by reading the Bible, but let's flesh out that concept a little more. As Christians, we believe that the inspired Word of God is just that— *the Word of God*. Second Timothy 3:16–17 says, "All Scripture is God-breathed and is useful for teaching, rebuking, correcting and training in righteousness, so that the servant of God may be thoroughly equipped for every good work." I don't know about you, but if God breathed it, it's good enough for me. Therefore, if I have an idea that I think may be from God, I make certain that it is consistent with Scripture. And I mean Scripture on the whole, not one little random verse in the Old Testament where the Israelites burned down the villages and killed all the cattle.

Here are some issues I consider when comparing an idea to the Bible:

> ▶ Is this idea consistent with the gracious and loving person of Christ? If Jesus happened to be in the room with me, would He join my endeavor?
> ▶ Is the idea free of any sin, such as pride, greed, idolatry, or self-centered pigheadedness?
> ▶ Does it have even one aspect that is clearly out of line, biblically?

You get the idea. If you think God is telling you something, compare it to the Bible. If it doesn't match up, then it's not God. It's the crazy voices in your head. Ignore them and move along.

We need to combine our search of the Scriptures with prayer. When we pray, we take the general principles from the Bible and begin to apply them to our personal experiences. We can ask God for wisdom, for help, and for provision. We can talk with the Creator of the universe about our daily, minute-by-minute experiences! First Thessalonians 5:16–18 says, "Rejoice always, pray continually, give thanks in all circumstances; for this is God's will for you in Christ Jesus." When are we supposed to be talking to God? Always! At all times!

But here's where the rubber hits our road, metaphorically speaking. Here's where this entire book becomes a real and personal thing—God communicates right back to us! He is alive, interested in every detail, and involved in every moment. Not only is He still involved but He still also has something to say. As we've discussed, He still calls us to projects, big and small. He also gives us wisdom for things the Bible doesn't address specifically. Things like, "Lord, should I let my kids ride the bus, or are they just learning too many naughty words on the way home from school?" Things like, "Lord, should I marry my boyfriend or become a single missionary to the Congo?" He can also speak comfort to us in our pain, and He can be a constant companion.

))) **"If you love me, keep my commands. And I will ask the Father, and he will give you another advocate to help you and be with you forever—the Spirit of truth"** **(John 14:15–17).**

This is all a gift of the Holy Spirit. As Jesus was leaving earth, He told the disciples that the Advocate would come. "But the Advocate, the Holy Spirit, whom the Father will send in my name, will teach you all things and will remind you of everything I have said to you" (John 14:26). I could probably write a thousand-page book about what it means to hear God speak—and still not cover it all. But I will say this: When I've been reading the Bible and praying, I have thoughts in my heart and mind that are different from my own thoughts. It feels as if someone else is in my mind, communicating with me exactly like a human friend would. Over the years I've learned that voice; I recognize it. Jesus said that His sheep follow Him because they know His voice (John 10:3–4), and I'm telling you that it is still possible to know and listen to Him. The voice is consistent with the written Word and undeniably the voice of the Almighty.

So, to summarize—unusual thoughts come into in my head. Thoughts I know don't come from myself, because I would never remind myself to be quiet and listen patiently. Nope, I pretty much tell myself to do whatever I want. I would never tell myself to trust God in a difficult situation, because my self tells myself to go ahead and take charge because God must not be on the job. It takes practice to recognize God's voice, but Jesus told us that His sheep will recognize Him when He speaks. Do we know our Shepherd? Are we as smart as sheep?

Who Wants a Whole Night of Sleep, Anyway?

When I think of the Lord speaking to us, I am reminded of the story of Samuel, found in 1 Samuel 3. As a child in Sunday school, I loved this Bible story. I find it encouraging to think that God spoke through a child to give a message to an elderly and respected priest. Even before Samuel's birth, God worked in his life. Samuel's birth was a miracle. His mother, Hannah, had been unable to conceive and had suffered ridicule from the other wife in the house. She lifted her broken heart to God and asked to have a son, and she promised to give that son to the work of the Lord. When God answered her prayer, Hannah was true to her word. She brought Samuel to the house of the Lord, or tabernacle, at a young age and left him to be raised there, dedicated to God's house. God spoke directly to Samuel and gave him the responsibility of sharing the message.

Now, Eli had been a priest for many years, but he had two

sons who were out of control. They were violating the sacrificial rites and sleeping with the women who served in the tabernacle. They were such evil men that God couldn't let them continue to make such horrible choices. Eli knew this was occurring—the gossip line was alive and well even in those days. A prophet even came to him to warn him directly from the Lord (1 Samuel 2:27–36). For some reason Eli failed to restrain his sons, and that was the final straw for God.

One night while Samuel and Eli were trying to fall asleep, God called Samuel. The boy was young enough that he didn't automatically assume it was God, so he trotted into Eli's room. Three times this happened, and finally Eli realized that God was calling. He told the little boy to say, "Speak, LORD, for your servant is listening" (1 Samuel 3:9). That is exactly what Sam did. Then God gave Samuel an unpleasant message, and he dreaded sharing it with Eli. But Eli knew that God's message was important, no matter what the consequences were. So he encouraged Samuel to share the word from the Lord.

I notice several things about this story. First, I find it interesting that God chose a child to deliver this message. Surely there were older and wiser men available who He could have chosen. But Samuel's heart was young and tender. He was able to hear the message clearly and deliver it accurately. An adult might have glossed over the unpleasant facts when relaying the word to Eli, saying, "Hey, Eli! God isn't happy with your boys. You might want to talk to them today." But Samuel told Eli exactly what God said.

Second, I notice that God was patient when calling Samuel and called him several times. How many times do you get a thought in your head, and you think, "Well, that's weird. What business do I have quitting this job and staying home with the kids?" And you go about your life. And then the thought comes again, and the sermon on Sunday is about sacrificing personal goals for the will of God, and your husband* has a meltdown because the kids are out of control and there is no dinner or clean socks, and the daycare calls because your kid has blackened someone's eye . . . and finally you realize the thrumming in your head may actually be God asking you to quit your job and stay home with the kids. God is patient with us. And let's face it, His timing rarely runs on American Standard Microwave Time. A day is like a thousand years to Him, so He's got the time to wait for us to get the message. His patience is legendary!

In her book *He Speaks to Me*, Priscilla Shirer discusses God patiently calling Samuel. She writes, "Be encouraged if the idea of hearing God's voice is new for you. It was new for Samuel too. Remember that God had to call Samuel three times. If you don't get it the first time, God will call again."[1] So true! God knows our hearts; He can tell if we're trying to get the message in our own limited, human way, and He will work with us until we do get it.

Third, Samuel was in a place where he could hear the voice of God in the first place. He was quiet, and he was able to hear and listen. I find it helpful to take time out to sit and listen to God when I think I'm getting a message. I will rarely hear correctly if I'm in the car, running carpool. My son and nephew will be fighting over who is over the imaginary line in the backseat, my daughter will be asking me what we're having for dinner, and the DJ on the radio will be announcing important traffic jams. I can't handle all that chaos and listen to God at the same time. Now, late at night when the kids are in bed and my husband is reading—that's when I can sit and listen to God. He's even spoken to me while I've been dusting, puttering around the kitchen, or taking a walk. But I need a quiet spirit so I can hear the message, because a quiet spirit is able to hear God. A noisy spirit can only

* Or wife. It's not 1954 anymore.

hear itself. Psalm 37:7 reminds us to "Be still before the LORD and wait patiently for him."

)))   **A quiet spirit is able to hear God. A noisy spirit can only hear itself.**

Sometimes it takes several days or attempts. I like to be up and doing things, lest I fall asleep. It can be painful to be sitting and concentrating on someone I can't see or audibly hear, but God knows that and He humors me. It appears that sometimes He's just testing to see how long I can sit still. (It's about five minutes.)

Sometimes the Voices in My Head Mimic the Voice of God

There is an extreme danger in believing we can hear the call of God—sometimes we don't know for sure that it is God speaking to us. In fact, sometimes it is definitely *not* God speaking, but we blame whatever crazy plan we have on Him anyway. Many ridiculous things have been done throughout history, and often the perpetrator will look everyone in the eye and claim the lunacy in the name of Christ. This gives us an offensive odor to the entire world, and I'm sure it doesn't make God happy in the least.

I think of the Crusades, forced conversions, the Holocaust, crosses burned in yards, abortionists murdered, homosexuals being beaten, or protestors picketing the funerals of soldiers. Certainly Christ abhors sin, but you've never heard of Jesus assaulting people because they refused to follow biblical commands. Think back to the scene when the soldiers came to arrest Him. One of the agitated disciples cut off a soldier's ear. Jesus rebuked him and healed the ear with a simple touch of His hand (Luke 22:50–51). He is compassionate and patient with people, waiting for them to come to Him willingly. We need to follow His example.

On the other hand, in this very book we're learning about some of the amazing things God has done, and frankly, some of them don't fit our modern approach. Take Abraham and Isaac, for example. If today Abraham tied up a child and attempted to sacrifice him, we'd have him in prison faster than a ram could be found (Genesis 22:1–18). In another example, the disciples often healed people and drove demons out. I know that can still be done today, but it isn't part of my daily routine. So how do we really know? What separates God's true plan from craziness? What if the voices are really just in my head and not the voice of the Almighty?

God Gave You a Noodle to Use

Ah, common sense. Some of us are born with so much of it that we hog the earth's fair share. My husband tells me that I have been practical since I was born, and this is true. I'm loath to run willy-nilly into any situation that doesn't make sense. Mind you, my common sense and wit are my only intellectual advantages, so I'm not getting a big head here. I couldn't be a doctor to save my life—or yours either, for that matter.

But back to my point. God gave us all a brain, and we need to use what He gave us as thoroughly as possible. Some ideas may fit biblically, but they are so crazy that we have no business blaming the ensuing catastrophe on God. If the people around you give you funny looks and say, "Really? What made you think of that?" you may want to slow down and think it through a bit more. You may want to ask a few more people and then realistically sit down and consider the consequences.

Let's revisit an earlier example of teaching a class of pre-schoolers at church. You may really be hearing God asking you to take that responsibility, even though you are a seventy-year-old woman who hasn't been near a preschooler in forty years. What are the consequences if you teach the class? Probably nothing earth-shattering. You may be a rusty teacher, but you'll do your best, and you and the kids will bumble along together, learning the Bible as best as you can. Anyone can take Play-Doh and make a snake and an apple. Bingo—first lesson!

However, what if you are that same seventy-year-old woman, and you feel that God is asking you to take your life savings, sell the house, and invest in a new business your grandson just thought up? The consequences of that decision are far more dire. Unless you are confident that you can live in that grandson's house and eat his food and use his electricity until you die, you may want to reconsider. God's requests rarely put His people in predicaments where they are financially, emotionally, or physically wiped out. And when His requests may indeed involve poverty, bodily harm, or ridicule, I believe His call is so clear that it is impossible to ignore what He is asking.

When Using Your Noodle Is Actually Ignoring God

Now we need to talk about when God really does ask for something that defies common sense. I think of Moses, Noah, the apostles, and even Paul. There is no common sense in leading thousands of stubborn Israelites on a meandering path through the desert for forty years. There is no sense involved in building an ark and waiting for animals—and rain—to show up. There is no sense in living a life of poverty, repeated imprisonments, and eventual martyrdom. But each of those men was filled with the Spirit and convinced that there was no other way to live. They knew that God was using them for something bigger than themselves, and it didn't matter how much it cost or how much they lost. The ultimate goal was bigger than their common sense.

A few years ago our friends Ben and Kris decided to sell their house and build a bigger one. And by *build one*, I mean that Ben himself got out a hammer and a ladder and starting making pieces of wood stick together with nails and things. The house is still standing several years later, which just goes to show what a determined man can do with a hammer. Reach for your dreams, my dear readers! If Ben can do it, so can you!

But back to the house. It had a really great floor plan. In fact, the floor plan was a bit roomy for two adults, two small children, and a dog. Ben is a campus minister, and he and Kris thought perhaps they could fill the extra two bedrooms with college students who needed a place to rent during the school year.

It wasn't long after they took possession of the new house that Kris started hearing God whisper about adoption. She and Ben started researching the advantages of international versus domestic adoption; babies versus older children. Kris was overcome with the needs of children everywhere, but for some reason the children in Ethiopia grabbed her heart the fiercest. She was unable to ignore the poverty and the struggle children are facing there.

Ben and Kris started making plans to adopt from Ethiopia. The cost was enormous—nearly $30,000. They planned, saved, prayed, sold possessions, and asked friends and family to help. Well, their new batch of children have been here with them for several years now, and we are all confident that this was exactly what God asked them to do.

Let's summarize all the ways Ben and Kris could have talked some sense into themselves and completely ignored God's plan. They could have had more biological children. They could have adopted from the American foster care system and saved a ton of money. Plus they would have saved themselves a trip to Ethiopia and the cultural challenges of international adoption. Picking up children from Africa is not the most logical way to fill up a house, people.

Yet they did it anyway. They stepped out in faith and followed God's call for their lives. If they had ignored God's call, who knows what would have happened to their adoptive children? If they had done this on their own strength, what would have happened to their family? The strain would have been too great, both for themselves and their finances. This required faith and discernment, step-by-step walking with God to get all the details as He released them—not running off on their own understanding to handle the situation.

All these options can be mind-boggling. We fear we'll miss God's voice because we aren't listening well enough. Maybe we fear hearing voices that aren't His. Maybe we have a great idea but we aren't sure of God's timing, and we worry that it will all blow up in our faces. Perhaps we hesitate because we don't want to do it on our own strength and end up with $50,000 in credit card bills and exhaustion to the max. But when we listen to God carefully, we'll hear clearly what He is saying. His leading will not lead us to destruction; it only leads us to what glorifies Him.

Our God Does Not Fit in Any Box We Have Yet Found

Let's take a step back here and find God's perspective. What we can see is only a portion of what is going on in relation to the whole world, to history, and to God's eternity.

Taking that concept, let's think about why God may be asking us to do something that appears to make no sense. If we think that everything we see and know is all there is, we are deluded. We don't even know what's going on in the minds of our closest family members, so how can we think that our opinion should have any effect on the known universe? Seriously, my husband is sitting about ten feet from me as I write this. I have no idea what is going on in his head. Is he mentally reviewing our finances?

Planning on buying me a new couch for my birthday? I don't know. And I probably don't want to know, frankly.

))) **"No eye has seen, no ear has heard, and no mind has imagined what God has prepared for those who love him" (1 Corinthians 2:9 NLT).**

But God sees everything, frontward, backward, and eternally—all at the same time. His limitless understanding makes our puny perspective seem almost laughable. First Corinthians 2:9 says, "No eye has seen, no ear has heard, and no mind has imagined what God has prepared for those who love him" (NLT). We can't imagine what God has planned, so we might as well sit back and enjoy it. We need to move beyond our limited views and embrace the reality that God may be asking us to do something surprising. Mind you, it will always be consistent with His Word, but it may turn your world upside down.

So if our hearts are tuning out God, refusing to listen because His words do not make sense to our understanding, perhaps we need to stop for a moment and consider what God can see that we cannot. What He knows that we cannot understand. What He wants that we haven't considered. Our lives may be used for something far greater than what we can see. Are we willing to let Him use us for His purposes?

Tuning Back In

We humans naturally rely on our senses and our common sense. Generally speaking, that's what keeps us alive from day to day. The topic of listening to God can be hard to discuss because it defies all our senses and most of our common sense. It requires that we develop a quiet heart that tunes into a frequency that others might not hear. It might make us sound like psychic loonies from a late night TV ad to them. Others may think we're trying to be too holy for our own good. But I think that if we could talk to Samuel, Moses, Noah, and Paul, they would tell us differently. Look at those early men of God, and consider what would have happened if they wouldn't have listened.

Jesus said that His sheep know His voice—can you hear Him calling?

STUDY QUESTIONS

1. How often do you hear from God? What are you doing (or not doing) when you hear Him?
2. What is a quiet and teachable spirit?
3. Have you developed a quiet spirit that is able to concentrate on God's Word and the Holy Spirit's direction? What did you do to develop that ability?
4. What distractions do you need to remove from your life so you can hear God frequently and consistently?
6. Are your plans consistent with Scripture?
7. Have you consulted a mature Christian about your plans?
8. Look up the following Scripture passages and apply them to your situation:
   a. Psalm 95:6–9
   b. Luke 10:38–42
   c. John 14:15–17, 26

Is This the Call of God?
or
Have I Gone Mad?

When God starts to speak to us, it can take a few tries before we really *get it*. Just like Samuel, we might attribute those thoughts or circumstances to something other than God's voice. Here are a few steps to help sort out your jumble of thoughts and emotions.

Ask Yourself:

▶ How many times has this thought come to me recently? Is it too often to be coincidence?

▶ Have I discussed this with my spouse? Will he or she be supportive? What are my spouse's concerns, and what would God need to provide to overcome them?

▶ What concrete things would we have to do to make this happen? Are we financially able, living in the right place, or working the right jobs? What would have to change?

▶ What are my strengths, weaknesses, and passions? Does this idea fit with anything God has designed me to do?

▶ How will this affect everyone around us? Have we considered the needs of our kids and extended family? Am I willing to trust God's direction and provision for our loved ones and act anyway?

▶ What sacrifices would we have to make? Am I willing to make them with a good attitude?

▶ Is this the right time? If we think it's not the right time, could it be the right time in God's eyes anyway?

▶ Have I taken the time to pray about all of my concerns, study the Bible, and wait for God to answer?

Next Steps:

▸ Sit down with your spouse and work through the finances. What will this cost? Consider *every cost imaginable*, both now and in the future. Do you feel God's peace even when the numbers might not add up? Pray over the finances.

▸ Make sure you understand your strengths and passions. Take some online personality tests like the DISC assessment and a spiritual gifts test. Prayerfully consider how God designed you and how this idea matches your gifts and abilities. Is it a good fit?

▸ Work out a timeline for any changes you need to make. List everything that needs to be done. Pray over the timeline.

▸ Study everything you can find about this new journey with God. Google it until your eyes are crossed. Talk to people who have done it before. Pray that God will give you wisdom and all the information you need. Pray that you will know when to stop seeking information and to start trusting God to work. ▪

CHAPTER 5

Getting the Timing and Directions Right

LUKE 6:46–49

Why do you call me, "Lord, Lord," and do not do what I say? As for everyone who comes to me and hears my words and puts them into practice, I will show you what they are like. They are like a man building a house, who dug down deep and laid the foundation on a rock. When a flood came, the torrent struck that house but could not shake it, because it was well built. But the one who hears my words and does not put them into practice is like a man who built a house on the ground without a foundation. The moment the torrent struck that house, it collapsed and its destruction was complete.

It is one thing to finally realize that God has a specific thing for you to do. It is yet another thing to get that job done correctly. It's not enough to hear from God; we must also get the right directions and follow them exactly, with the right timing.

Let's say we want to bake a pan of brownies. We dig out the cookbook and read that we need cocoa, oil, sugar, eggs, flour, and baking soda. Then we have to mix it all up and bake it for thirty minutes. We open up the cupboard and fridge, and we don't have any of those things. So we dig out some sausage, croutons, a tub of butter, and the garlic seasoning. We combine it and bake for an hour. Well, super. You can pull that pan out of the oven and call it brownies, but what you really have is stuffing.

Every woman in the northern hemisphere knows that when

you're needing brownies, stuffing isn't going to cut it. You've got to get it all right, or it's all wrong. We can do that with God's call too.

The trick here is reading the recipe God hands you so you *can* follow it exactly. If there is one thing that paralyzes me from completing what I know I'm supposed to do, it is not knowing exactly how I'm supposed to get the job done. It's like opening a box and finding that your toaster comes in three hundred parts. You dig out the instructions, and all it says is, "Assemble pieces until bread is as crisp as you like it." Sometimes I feel as if God's directions can be a bit vague, which leads to all kinds of trouble. If I'm really excited about the project, I might dive right in and mess everything right up. If I'm not so excited about the assignment, I might take my sweet time and hijack God's plan by my dawdling. You see how this can get complicated.

A few years ago I was at one of our local superstores, doing my grocery shopping. I noticed a man pushing a cart; his young daughter was riding in the front seat. I knew I was supposed to give him twenty dollars. Clear as a bell, I knew that was what I was supposed to do. And heaven help me, I followed that man around the store for half an hour. I wasn't right behind him, mind you, so he never suspected that a nut job was trying to figure out a way to slip him some cash. I really didn't know how to get him the money. If I walked right up to him and handed him the cash, I was afraid I would offend or embarrass him. I thought about tucking the money into the cart, but I wasn't sure how to make it stick before it fell out. I thought about asking him if he had dropped it in hopes that he would claim it, but somehow tricking a man into lying for the sake of God's twenty bucks seemed a bit twisted. Finally, I gave up and went on with the grocery shopping, hoping to get a brilliant idea. As I was finishing, I saw him again. Now he and the girl had a few pet supplies in the basket, and I was stumped. Why would God want me to give money to people who were buying unnecessary stuff? They obviously had money someplace. So I decided that the idea was crazy and I was not really hearing God. I paid for my groceries and left the store.

I'll tell you, it's been more than six years since then, and I still know I should have given that man the twenty dollars. If I had the same situation today, I would walk right up to him, hand him the money, say that God told me he needed it, and walk away. I would then go to another aisle where I would try not to have a nervous fit. But I would do it. Six years ago I really messed the whole thing up, and I hope like crazy that another Christian was in that store with more guts to do what God needed for that man. I got the assignment loud and clear, my attitude was right, but my follow-through was a disaster.

Lucky for you, we don't have to depend just on my long-winded stories to prove a point. We're going to discuss Jonah and Esther, two people from the *Bible*. Jonah had issues with following directions, and Esther had a huge, vague project assigned to her and needed some help in the timing department. In the end, though, I think it was their attitudes that really determined the outcomes. Let's take a look at our ancient friends to see what we can learn from their lives, shall we?

Jonah: AKA Defiant Man Who Smells Like Fish

Jonah, the lucky old dog, actually got a clear recipe handed to him right from God. "Go to the great city of Nineveh," God said, "and preach against it, because its wickedness has come up before me" (Jonah 1:2). In a mind-numbing act of outright defiance, Jonah picked another direction and attempted to flee from the Lord. Jonah 1:3 actually says that he "sailed for Tarshish to flee from the LORD." Not "flee from this uncomfortable job." Or "he disagreed with God's supporting arguments and removed himself from the situation." No, he tried to hide from God.

"Um, duuuuu-uuuuh," we say, all smug with ourselves several thousands of years later. You got a clear order from the Lord, and you did completely the opposite. How'd that work out for ya, Jonah?

Badly. It always works out badly when you know what you're supposed to do and you don't do it. It may be as simple as a haunting regret that you can't shake regarding twenty dollars. It may be something that destroys your relationships with family or friends. It might be a long, nasty trip covered in fish guts until you get puked out on the sand—and *then* you do exactly what God wanted you to do in the first place.

It's better to obey and do what God wants, *without* the nasty fish-ride. The second time, Jonah did it right. God gave him a second chance, and he obeyed the directions exactly. He went to Nineveh, he told them God's message, and lo and behold—everyone listened! Families were changed! Lives were spared! God was pleased! "When God saw what they did and how they turned from their evil ways, he relented and did not bring on them the destruction he had threatened" (Jonah 3:10).

Jonah wasn't pleased, however. He was a grumpy old goat with a bad attitude, and the book of Jonah drops off suddenly in the middle of God's lecture. We never get to find out if he changed his mind and was thankful that the Ninevites were spared. It just ends after his snit and a time-out under a dead vine. (Always remember that a good attitude should accompany obedience. Otherwise, you might get an embarrassing book about yourself added to the Bible—just to prove God's point.)

I'm thankful that the story of Jonah was included in the Old Testament. What a clear testimony of what can happen when we refuse to follow God's directions! We've all been warned, and we have Jonah's terrible choices and attitudes to thank for that.

Esther: Queen Holy-Cow-What's-Going-On-Here?

Oh, poor little Esther. Really, what woman plans on being orphaned, winning a beauty pageant, marrying the king as the prize, and then being the only person who can save her entire people group? This is the sort of plot we find in cheesy movies-of-the-week. It's a lot to put on a real woman's shoulders. But Esther did it—and without clear directions like Jonah had.

I won't go into the whole story of Esther, because it can get kind of convoluted and confusing unless you have the time to tell the whole thing properly. We're going to pick up in Esther 4, when Esther's cousin Mordecai went to her and told her that Haman, a government official, was going to kill all the Jews. Mordecai relayed through a messenger that Esther, who was the queen, needed to go to the king, beg for mercy, and plead with him for her people.

Esther sent the messenger back to her cousin with a reminder that just waltzing into the king's presence got you D-E-A-D dead—unless he offered you the scepter. And everyone knows that a dead queen can't beg for mercy for her people. So it was kind of a backward plan.

Mordecai sent the messenger back with a few key points (4:12–14). He said Esther would die too, simply because she was a Jew. Living in the king's house wasn't going to change her fate. He added that remaining silent would cause deliverance to come from another place, but that she and her family would still likely die. And also, perhaps dear Esther was granted this royal position for such a time as this! She got to be the queen to *save her people*, not to have an excellent selection of tunics and eunuchs.

Esther was still in a bind. She knew beyond a shadow of a

doubt that the responsibility fell to her. It was her destiny. But doing it was going to get her killed unless something intervened. For the life of her, she didn't know what to do. So she sent word to Mordecai again that he was to gather all the Jews in Susa and fast for her for three days. She and her maids would fast as well, and after the three days she would go into the king. If she died, she died. At least she would have died doing her best.

Skipping to the end of the story, we see that Esther took her time and finessed the king. We have to remember that they were married but really didn't have a close relationship. So, before she made her request, she had a few dinners with him, she made him feel all warm and special, and then she finally spit out what she needed. At that point she had the king's attention, and he acted on her behalf.

This is the benefit of doing things with God's timing. It may take time to fast and seek God's blessing. It may take time to develop relationships with people. If Esther had rushed into the king's room without taking the time to fast and without the Jews fasting with her, the results may have been disastrous. She may have been executed before she could get the message out. Waiting on God's timing is always better than getting yourself killed, I feel.

A few years ago I was having a minor panic attack about *my entire life.* Suddenly the idea of becoming a writer had moved from fantasy to distinct possibility as my manuscript moved through the approval process at the publishing house. I need to emphasize once again that I have fallen into this calling like one might fall off a log and then roll down a mountain, or like one might get hit by a bus while trying to cross a street. *I never saw it coming. I was not prepared.*

Once I started to research what being an author meant, I went from minor panic attack to full-blown hysteria. Do you know how many options are available to a writer these days? Nonfiction or fiction books. Blogging or not blogging. Full speaking schedule or never leaving the house. Writing articles for magazines or penning devotionals for the women's group at church. In my panic I did something out of character—I emailed a complete stranger and asked for help.

Cynthia Heald writes Bible studies. She's known for her Becoming a Woman of . . . series, and I own several of these books and reread them every couple of years. I knew she writes and speaks, so I tracked that poor woman down through email and begged for advice. "How do I do this?" I asked.

The dear woman called me on the phone. *She called me!* There's nothing quite as surreal as a voicemail message from a woman whose work you've been reading for years. I called her back as soon as the kids were in bed, and she calmed me down with this quote out of *My Utmost for His Highest,* a devotional by Oswald Chambers. The March 11 reading says this:

> Watch for the storms of God. The only way God plants His saints is through the whirlwind of His storms. Will you be proved to be an empty pod with no seed inside? That will depend on whether or not you are actually living in the light of the vision you have seen. Let God send you out through His storm, and don't go until He does. If you select your own spot to be planted, you will prove yourself to be an unproductive, empty pod. However, if you allow God to plant you, you will "Bear much fruit" (John 15:8).

And that's exactly what we want, isn't it—to *bear much fruit?* Mrs. Heald and Mr. Chambers are right. If we want that fruit, we have to be planted where God wants us, and that means we wait for His timing, for His wind, for His planting. Mrs. Heald told me that God would make it clear and would bring opportunities when the timing was right. I calmed my hysterical self down, went back to mothering my children and cleaning my house, and waited for God to do His thing. The pressure was off me, and God could work without my interference. We both found this to be a better system. I think you might too.

The Consequences of Running Ahead of God's Timing

Unlike Esther's situation, there are few opportunities to gravely disappoint the king in modern life. Our consequences are far less dire but usually last a lot longer and may feel more painful than a quick execution. Here are a few things to think about, but my list is by no means exhaustive. There are plenty of other horrible things that can happen to you when you get an assignment from God and then rush on ahead without waiting for the directions:

> ▶ Financial Ruin—I am a firm believer that God always provides the resources when He gives someone a job to do. In fact, the next chapter of this book spends a lot of time on this exact subject. But I believe it deserves a note here, as well. If you are spinning your wheels on God's project and you're panicking because there's no money, then I think there is an issue with your timing or your understanding of the scope of the need. For example, you don't hear about Noah deciding to take four of each animal on board, and therefore doubling the size of the ark. He would have needed a credit card from his local Lowe's, and you know how they were about credit in those days. But he could have leveraged the family farm or maybe traded in a herd of sheep . . . No! God gave him a job, and

then God gave him the resources. He took the time to understand what was needed, and he built it exactly. God never asks us to ruin our credit, jeopardize our reputations, or borrow money to complete His work. He owns it all, and He'll release the funds as soon as they are needed. It's part of the awesome and terrifying and amazing miracle of working with God. Don't go running ahead of God and expect Him to pay off the credit card bill.

▶ Overworking Yourself—Have you ever watched a child attempt a job designed for a grown-up? It's exhausting. Sometimes my son tries to help me put clean sheets on the bed. He can't stretch the bottom sheet tightly enough. The top sheet gets stuck in the crack next to the wall. The blankets are all way too huge to spread out. And for little hands the pillowcase is impossible to wedge onto the pillow. He's trying, he wants to help, but the job just isn't designed for him. Now, when we do the job together, I can help him with the pillows and the huge linens. God's jobs for us are like that. If we try doing a God-sized job on our own, we're going to have a meltdown. We need to wait until He's right with us, giving us step-by-step directions.

▶ Missing the Point Altogether—It is entirely possible to go running about God's business like a chicken with its head cut off. You're moving, you look productive, but really nothing of value is being accomplished. Stop, wait for directions, and rest a minute. Maybe God has asked you to volunteer at your children's school because there is a specific child who needs you. But if you show up at 8:30 and run through the school helping five different teachers and making lunch and then driving the bus home, you might miss that one child in all the activity. But taking the time to ask God exactly what He is saying and attending to that one area will result in accomplishing exactly what He wants.

I'm Getting There, I'm Getting There

Maybe you read that last section and thought, "What are you talking about? Who would run ahead of God's directions?" I don't mean to be offensive, but I'm guessing that perhaps you're one who may be called a "Plodder." Or a "Slowpoke." Perhaps even a "Dawdler." It's no secret that some of us are built for high-octane movement and some of us are slow, steady, Sunday drivers. This is not a problem; I'm just saying that we need to be careful when it comes to acting on God's will. It is as dangerous to wait too long as it is to run ahead.

First, dawdling too long might get you left in the dust. God's timing may be far different from our own, but there is still a point when the line is crossed and the opportunity is over. First Thessalonians 5:2–3 tells us, "you know very well that the day of the Lord will come like a thief in the night. While people are saying, 'Peace and safety,' destruction will come on them suddenly, as labor pains on a pregnant woman, and they will not escape." We want to be ready before the thief comes, before the labor pains begin.

Second Coming aside, this concept is important in our lives right now too. For example, God always calls us to parent our children as wisely as possible. If you decide that parenting is too much work and wait until your son is thirty-three before you begin to discipline him, your opportunity is gone. You'll be the anguished parent of a selfish, adult-sized dunderhead who sees no need to restrain himself in any situation or for any reason. Yes, parenting is a lot of work, but the consequences of *not* parenting are too dire. We have to take the opportunity when it's there.

Second, and this is the far more important issue, is that sometimes our dawdling is actually a problem with quiet defiance. I think most of us have been with a child who has been told to put her shoes on so everyone can leave for dinner. The sweet monkey smiles and agrees, and then she slowly wanders over to the bookshelf and pulls out three books. You remind her again about the shoes and the leaving and the dinner, and she smiles again and disappears to the bathroom. You are now outside the bathroom door, throwing the shoes in at her, hoping she can catch them while sitting on the toilet. Your husband is in the car, honking the horn. The precious she-child washes her hands for fifteen minutes and comes out with wet socks.

This is where we have two options in our house: I begin shouting like a lunatic, or I pick up the child, take her out to the car, shoes in hand, and plop her bottom in the backseat. I slam the back door, and we haul. No one is happy, and it would have been so much easier for the kid to *just put on her shoes!* Please, don't do this to God. I'm not sure what He does when we frustrate him so badly, but the word *smite* comes to mind.

Third, sometimes we attempt to stall God's plan because we just don't trust Him. I encourage you to take several weeks to make a study of every biblical example used in this book. Each story represents a time when God asked His people to step out in faith and trust Him, and every single time He proved worthy of trust. *Every single time.* He will never leave you nor forsake you, and His promise is sure.

Besides, sitting on the couch, plugging your ears, and hoping that God forgets He asked you to do something is never a clever idea.

The Recipe Calls for Three Eggs and Thirty Minutes!

So, please remember. If God calls for brownies, you'll need to follow the recipe for brownies. Or, He may be asking for some wild and exotic dish you never dreamed of making, but He'll never leave you without the recipe. You need to ask Him and then wait until He gives you the answer. Remember Jonah, who decided that God's plan for Nineveh wasn't good? What happened to him? A long ride in a fish, that's what happened. Remember Esther, who finessed the king with dinners. Her people were saved because she did what needed to be done, with a keen sense of timing.

Your project with God can turn out either way. Fishy or perfect. You choose.

STUDY QUESTIONS

1. What clear directions has God given you so far?

2. Have you started anything yet? How has it turned out? What have you learned?

3. What part of His plan is still vague? How do you think God will relay the next steps?

4. Are you 100 percent committed to following God's plan exactly, with a good attitude? (Seriously, the only answer here is "yes." Remember Jonah?)

5. What are the consequences if you run ahead of God's schedule?

6. What are the consequences if you dillydally?

7. How much time have you spent with God to determine the instructions He is giving?

8. Look up the following Bible passages and consider what the consequences would have been if God's directions had not been followed exactly:

   a. Genesis 12:1–9
   b. Matthew 2:1–16

David Goes to University

There are people who claim that the Internet doesn't allow for real friendships to grow. I think they're wrong, because Eric and I met the Welfords through blogging. Even though they live in Great Britain, we regularly exchange parenting stories, weather reports, and general comments about one another's lives. Also, David graciously informs me when my American slang means something frightful to his British sensibility. That's happened more times than we have time to discuss right here,* because we have to get to his story about when he went to college.

I was twenty-eight years old at the time, married with two children, and about to leave my job to become a university student in Cardiff for three years. To do this I needed a grant from my local education authority (LEA), but I could not get anyone in the LEA to confirm in writing I would receive a grant, or how much it would be. Both were crucial to my handing in my notice, because my boss had asked for three months notice so he could recruit a replacement before I left.

At this stage everything had come together for me to go to University; it was just the finance I couldn't tie down. I couldn't believe I had been offered a place, because I had left school at sixteen. The University had accepted my professional qualifications as equivalent to the normal entry requirements. The entire summer after giving my notice at work was an exercise in trust right up until I arrived at the University in late September and collected my grant cheque [check!].

I had no choice but to step out in faith and trust God to meet

---

* For example, in the United States we use the word *pants* for anything we put on our legs to leave the house. But in the United Kingdom the word *pants* means "*under*pants." And one day I wrote a whole blog post about pants. It's a good thing the Brits have a sense of humor. Yikes!

the family's needs for the time I would be at University. In those days it wasn't so much a voice, just a deep knowledge that this was God leading me into the next phase of my life, but in doing that He needed one thing from me—He needed me to trust Him to provide for the family.

There were other issues that I had to seek God about. We could have moved. We didn't think this was right, so I commuted on a weekly basis during the school term. This obviously added to the costs and meant living apart as a family during the week. On the plus side it helped me focus on my studies. My wife, Marilyn, and my parents encouraged me and stood with me. One person in particular at church was also a source of continual encouragement.

Even with God's provision and the encouragement from family, there were many bumps. Living away from home during the week left Marilyn to cope alone with our two children (Nick and Michael aged five and three at the start of my course) while also working part-time. I used to catch a train Sunday afternoon and come home Thursday night some weeks, and Friday night other weeks. Then I worked all Saturday morning as a swimming instructor. So our family time was restricted in term time.

During the long University holidays we had more time, but I continued to work at the swimming pool so we could have sufficient funds. Then at the start of my third year, Marilyn became pregnant with our third son, James.

Even with the LEA grant and two part-time incomes, it was a massive struggle. There was a mortgage to pay at home and rent on my room in Cardiff where I lived during the week. The common sense thing we did was change to a lower-cost mortgage, and we tried to live within our means. That meant borrowing a tent and equipment from our neighbours to have a summer camping holiday in West Wales. It rained six days out of seven and damaged me to the extent that I promised myself I would never camp again.

What did God do? He never let us go without. I still really can't tell you how we survived those three years. I just don't know. Spiritually, I gained massively from being at Uni. I became part of a house group. I had never come across such a thing before. I found myself learning from Christians who were ten years younger than me. So the sacrifices of being away from family and living in student houses (the one in the second year was borderline squalid—slugs coming through the brickwork and slug trails across the floors!) were rewarded by spiritual growth the likes of which I had not experienced before.

And I eventually earned a degree! That led me into a new career and eventually into work as a self-employed consultant. That has made me more flexible, allowing me to be available to do more and different things in my church, although some of those demands are quite testing at times!

Nearly thirty years later, I can see how God's hand was on my life then and how the return to education was part of His plan and enabled me to become the person I am now for Him. Given the wonderful science of hindsight, I can look back and see what He has achieved despite my weaknesses, my lack of faith, and my attitude. Why is it so difficult to trust God for His provision in all things? Why does the lesson have to be repeated so many times? God's strength is continually worked out through my weaknesses.

I had many fears going off to University as a twenty-eight-year-old. I didn't know how we would manage as a family or how I would manage as a student. Generally, I am a very risk-averse person. I don't easily step out of the boat. But I know that when God wants me to do something I have to get out of the boat, where the only possibility of survival is to keep my eyes on Him and trust that He will reach out and catch my hand if I look down and start to sink.

I actually think that fear is good. It means that we are not doing stuff in our strength if we have fear to keep us grounded. I'd rather be afraid than overconfident in my own abilities. As it happened we all survived. I graduated with honours. And long-term we all benefited as a family and continue to do so. ■

CHAPTER 6

Preparing Financially

2 CORINTHIANS 9:6-8

Remember this: Whoever sows sparingly will also reap sparingly, and whoever sows generously will also reap generously. Each of you should give what you have decided in your heart to give, not reluctantly or under compulsion, for God loves a cheerful giver. And God is able to bless you abundantly, so that in all things at all times, having all that you need, you will abound in every good work.

How many times does God ask us to do something that involves money, resources, or time? Has He *ever* asked us to do something that doesn't involve those things? We humans tend to think that money, resources, and time are ours. They aren't! They're God's! I think He reminds us of this every time we use them for Him. Whether He's asked you to build houses in Guatemala or quit your job to stay home with the children or move your mother into your home, money is going to figure into your ability to accomplish His assignment for you. And especially in the modern world, the financial cost can be a stumbling block that stops us from jumping right into the project.

I touched on this in the last chapter, but here it is again in bigger font:

God Always Provides the Resources When He Asks Us to Do Something!!

Really, I can't tell you how strongly I feel about this. It's a terrible feeling to be staring down the barrel of an empty checking account while bills pile up on the table. It's no fun to look into the future at expenses you know are waiting for you—without any clue of how you will pay for them when the time comes. But if God is really behind what you are doing, the money is going to be there. It just is.

We see an excellent example of this principle in the Old Testament when David and Solomon prepared to build the temple. You can find the story in 1 Chronicles 28 through 2 Chronicles 4. This project was so huge that it took two kings and years of planning, years of donations, years of storing the donations, and finally, years of actually building the temple. King David pointed out in 1 Chronicles 29:1 that "the task is great, because this palatial structure is not for man but for the LORD God."

First Chronicles 29 tells us about the financial aspect of building the temple. King David had allocated resources to build the temple, and he also threw in a great deal of his own personal wealth. Then the Jewish leaders added from their personal savings. And everyone was thrilled to do it! It was God's project, and His people were pleased to be able to contribute. David said in verse 14: "But who am I, and who are my people, that we should be able to give as generously as this? Everything comes from you, and we have given you only what comes from your hand."

In 2 Chronicles 3 we see why all that money was needed. This wasn't some floppy, old backwoods tent. This was a huge project. It was beautiful. The finest and fanciest resources were used to build the structure; then workers coated it in gold. Chapter 4 discusses the mind-boggling furnishings for the temple, which included tongs made of solid gold. Solid. Gold. Tongs. Try registering for those at Target. Keep those tongs in mind when you're wondering if God is going to provide for the project He's assigned you.

))) **If God provided solid gold tongs for the temple, He can provide for those bills on my table.**

Waiting for God to Provide

I notice that as David and Solomon prepared to build the temple they put a great deal of time and thought into the blueprints and the financing. They worked for years to set aside the funds and resources needed to complete a building worthy of the presence of the Almighty. This ties into the previous chapter when we discussed moving with God's timing. If David had charged into the project before it was time, the plans wouldn't have been complete. The money would not have been there. Therefore, the project would not have been nearly as grand nor what God had in mind.

Please, please consider any debt very carefully when you dive into God's project. The temple was a huge financial undertaking, and it does not say anywhere that David or Solomon borrowed any money from anyone. Gifts were given. Resources were saved. Sacrifices were made. But no one borrowed any money! Debt must always be paid back, and we might not be in a financial state to pay it back later. We cannot presume upon God's plans for the future.

The Past Comes Back to Bite Us

You may be nodding your head right now because you are keenly aware that presuming upon God's plans for the future is a bad idea. You know this because you're living right now with the consequences from yesterday, even from years ago. Student loans pop into my head as a handy example. It seemed so simple when I was a young lass of eighteen. I signed on the dotted line, I cheerfully agreed to repay those loans, and I went off to class. Fortunately, I've always been leery of debt, and I limited the amount I borrowed. I could have left college with $40,000 in loans, but I managed to squeak out with around $8,000. I worked a lot of hours at my off-campus job, ate a lot of macaroni and cheese, and begged my parents for a lot of rent money.

Even with those preventive measures, it still took Eric and me almost eight years to pay off that debt. It's really, *really* hard to pay off student loans when you have a house payment and two babies. Eric had student loans of his own, so we ended up working opposite shifts for years so we could pay off the debts and not need to pay for day care. *It was horrible.* We saw each other for about fifteen minutes a day—as I was coming home and he was heading into work. Our conversations went like this: "Audrey napped from one to three this afternoon, but she hasn't had a snack. She's watched two episodes of *Sesame Street*. Caleb hasn't pooped yet today. I love you, good-bye."

God was gracious to us; it appears our only calling at that point in our lives was to (1) survive and (2) pay off debt so we could be ready for what He called us to next. Here's the really great news—we did pay off all our combined student loans, and then we were free to move ahead with God's plan, whatever that was. And surprise of all surprises, His plan was to have me write some books. Who knew? The early years of writing generally involve zero income, so it was critical that we were able to live on one salary. There's no way we could have done it with those loans hanging around our necks.

))) **If we want to be free to obey God when He calls, we must do our best to make choices now that aren't going to truss us up like the Christmas goose later.**

I tell you this story for two reasons. First, I love to tell long and pointless stories. But more than that, I also want to help you look clearly into the future. The choices we all made yesterday are affecting us today, and the choices we make today are going to affect tomorrow. If we want to be free to obey God when He calls, we must do our best to make choices now that aren't going to truss us up like the Christmas goose later. Hebrews 12:1–2 says:

> Therefore, since we are surrounded by such a great cloud of witnesses, let us throw off everything that hinders and the sin that so easily entangles, and let us run with perseverance the race marked out for us. Fixing our eyes on Jesus, the pioneer and perfecter of faith. For the joy set before him he endured the cross, scorning its shame, and sat down at the right hand of the throne of God.

We need to "throw off everything that hinders," so we are able to run the race God has marked out for us! Paul then goes on to tell us exactly how to do this—we focus on Jesus, who ran His own race with perfection and sacrifice. Jesus was focused on the joy before Him in heaven, not worldly things like houses, careers, or vacations to Bermuda. He had the right focus and the right attitude about sacrifice. Do we?

Yikes, Lady. How Old *Are* You? Do You Know How Much Things Cost Now?

Isn't it adorable how a year of college cost $10,000 in 1995? I realize you may be attending a college that costs $30,000-plus a year. You spend more in books each semester than I spent in macaroni and cheese for four years. Perhaps you are already past the college years but are considering house and car purchases, prices for which are out of control. *Think carefully. Choose wisely.* What is your priority—being able to obey God whenever He calls, or having that fancy degree/four-bathroom house/van with the heated leather seats? Let's go back to our earlier discussion. God always provides the resources when He asks us to do something, but the choices we make can really gum up the works.

Let's say that one day God calls you to be a missionary in Cambodia. Let's say that before this happens you get a master's degree from a private university and have student loans of over $100,000. I just ran the numbers through a financial loan calculator, and if we assume a ten-year repayment schedule and 6 percent interest, the payment each month will be $1,110.21.[1] You would need a yearly salary of $133,000 to pay this back assuming that 10 percent of your gross income is dedicated to your student loans.

Just for the record, missionaries to Cambodia do not make $133,000 a year.

Think for a moment of what it would be like to try to raise support to go to Cambodia with monthly student loan payments of $1,110. How would you explain that to supporters? Can you feel the stress that obligation would place on your ability to follow God's call? It's not just student loans that slow us down either. Credit card debt, enormous houses, car payments for fancy vehicles, furniture sets, vacations—those suckers can all sink us.

Of course, we serve a God big enough to handle our problems and get the work done that He needs done. If He could get a million stubborn Hebrews out of Egypt, He can take care of the choices you made five years ago. He's looking for willing hearts, not perfect track records. In fact, this enormous financial problem might be just another way for Him to show His strength with a miracle. Jeremiah 32:27 sums it up aptly: "I am the LORD, the God of all mankind. Is anything too hard for me?" As we move forward into the calling God has for us, we have to believe the answer to His question is *no*. There's nothing too hard for God.

))) **"I am the LORD, the God of all mankind. Is anything too hard for me?" (Jeremiah 32:27)**

Okay, but I Do Need an Education and a Place to Live

The obvious problem here is that many of us have no idea of what God may call us to in the future, but we still need to make choices about our present. It doesn't make a lot of sense not to go to college just because God might call you to Cambodia in five years. It's a little nutty to live in a two-bedroom apartment with your five children just because you don't want to have a mortgage in case He calls you to move across the country suddenly. There's nothing sinful about going to college, having a reasonable student loan if it's necessary, or owning a house. The key here is that we make these decisions prayerfully and carefully, fully aware that God's plans are not always our plans. Once again, God is looking for willing hearts. James 1:5 reminds us to ask God if we need wisdom, because He gives generously and without finding fault. He might not give us the exact plan for the future, but He certainly can help us make the good decisions now that will be a blessing when the time comes.

Get a Pen, Honey! We Need to Do Some Figuring

Waiting for God to provide is really challenging, and every assignment God gives is a little different. There's no easy formula to determine the financial possibilities or risks. There's no single verse that covers all financial matters in our journey with God. But we can do this—we can take our assignments to paper and figure the cost in every aspect. Here are a few thoughts to prayerfully and honestly address:

- ▸ How much cold, hard cash do you need to complete this? Perhaps you need to rework your family budget with a proposed salary, research the cost of college, or find the cost of living for a family of six in Honduras.
- ▸ What needs to change for you to reach this goal financially? Do you need to sell your home, keep the clunker car, or start saving more money?
- ▸ Is anyone else available to help with this project? God rarely assigns a project that doesn't involve the people around us. Perhaps your family or friends can contribute, or they know of an extra job that would provide the money.
- ▸ Is there still a shortfall after exhausting your personal resources, ideas, and friends' pockets? Take the difference to God. He can make up the difference.

I need to point out that I don't think borrowing money is evil. The Bible says that the "borrower is slave to the lender" (Proverbs 22:7), and it warns against financial foolishness. However, borrowing money intelligently can be a useful financial tool. The trick is to do your best not to get in over your head. For example, rarely can normal people plunk down enough cash to buy a house outright. But if you choose your home carefully so that your mortgage takes only a reasonable percentage of your family income, the borrowed money probably won't put you in bondage to your lender. You'll still be able to tithe, save for the future, and meet your family's needs. Also, if God calls you to the mission field or wants you to quit your job, you'll be able to sell the home and move along. This is not the case with $100,000 of credit card debt. You see the difference? A modest mortgage is simply wise use of a financial tool. Furnishing an entire house with Pottery Barn furniture financed on the VISA, however, is simply dumb, dumb, dumb.

))) **A modest mortgage is simply wise use of a financial tool. Furnishing an entire house with Pottery Barn furniture financed on the VISA is simply dumb, dumb, dumb.**

No One *Needs* Four Bathrooms—Unless God Is Asking You to Start an Orphanage

This is a painful section; let me prepare you. People in the Western world stink at recognizing our blessings and denying ourselves, and we are bombarded with messages that we need and deserve more than the abundance we already have.

I have an assignment for you—it's actually kind of fun. Go to the library and check out Laura Ingalls Wilder's book *Little House on the Prairie*. (Do not watch the TV show and expect it to be the same. You've got to read the book!) If you aren't into the whole pioneer thing, at least skip to the chapter where they finish the log house out on the prairie and move in. They had enough room for two beds, a crib, the fireplace, and a table. Perhaps they had a cupboard or something to store the few dishes they had. Their chairs were stumps. Pa went to town and brought back enough glass to put in the windows, and it was a fantastic luxury.

After you've read the book, put it down and turn on a few home shows. You know, the ones where the couple shops for a house and discovers that the one with four thousand square feet isn't quite right because the kitchen doesn't house a robot maid. Compare the difference between the Ingalls's prairie cabin and the four-thousand-square-foot suburban dream home. Doesn't something seem off with the new standards? Don't they make you feel kind of yucky? I need to confess that I love house shows, and they often suck me right in. I've actually had to limit my viewing to just a few shows a week, and even then sometimes I get carried away. When you soak your mind with TV luxury, reality can seem pretty drab.

However, when we surround ourselves with God's perspective, reality looks, well, real. The Bible reminds us over and over that we are aliens and strangers here on earth (1 Peter 2:11), and our goal is not to spend all our time and energy perfecting our short earthly stay. This requires that we scale our idea of "needs" back to what God considers a "need." He often gives us our wants, and hard work pays off more often than not. Many luxuries are the result of people who came along before us and used their brains and hard work to accomplish something great (thank you, whoever implemented citywide sewage systems).* But spend time researching how the vast majority of the world lives right now and how people have lived in the past. The truth will set you free!

My point is that sometimes we need to gear our minds toward what God knows we need, so we can free up our financial resources to get His job done. If four bathrooms and the robot maid are figured into the financial equation, you're going to get frustrated, because it will seem like God isn't providing. However, God's financial equation may include a tiny apartment with no cable TV so you can save $1,000 a month to get your student loans paid off by Easter and be on the mission field by the Fourth of July. Or adopt two Ethiopian babies. Or stay at home and write a book.

* I'd also like to take a moment to thank the inventors of hot water heaters, the automatic coffeepot with built-in timer, and electric blankets. Thank you, that is all.

Reaping and Sowing, Reaping and Sowing

I love to garden. I take those little seeds, I plop them into the soil, and I care for my little bit of earth. It all works together with a little bit of a miracle to create something amazing. Pumpkins, tomatoes, maple trees, zinnias—all the same deal. I sow the seed. I reap the end product.

The Bible points out several times that we reap what we sow, and finances are no different. Those who sow generosity reap generous rewards. Second Corinthians 9:10–11 says: "Now he who supplies seed to the sower and bread for food will also supply and increase your store of seed and will enlarge the harvest of your righteousness. You will be enriched in every way so that you can be generous on every occasion, and through us your generosity will result in thanksgiving to God." He gives to us generously so we can be generous to others; we can't be tempted to hoard the resources He's given us. In fact, your entire assignment may be to give the resources He's let you accumulate for a short time.

I know of a family who has been blessed with extreme financial wealth. You'd never know it, because they drive normal vehicles and work like perfectly normal people. They serve in quiet ways and eat with the commoners . . . normal stuff. Not only do they serve quietly but they also they give quietly. And not just a few dollars here and there, but in large and generous doses. Not once have they waltzed in and made demands in exchange for the money either. They give it and go about their business. It's their ministry and that's that. Oh, how their witness is a blessing to me and the very few others who know their whole story.

I know of another family who also gives generously, and for the life of me I don't know how they do it. The husband lost his job a few years ago and couldn't find steady or profitable employment for several years. But during that time they gave over a thousand dollars for a special missions fund, even when they were struggling to make ends meet most months. When God gave them an unexpected windfall, the bonus went right back out to ministry. They knew that sowing generously meant reaping generously, even if they had to wait until the next life to reap the reward. Like the widow with her two small coins (Mark 12:41–44), they shared what they had when they had it.

Your Financial Assignments

Getting the financial side right is crucial to accomplishing God's project. If you're still not certain that God can provide for your needs, here is a list of homework assignments that will bring God's perspective into focus:

▶ Read 1 Chronicles 28 and 29, and also 2 Chronicles 1–5. If your project seems overwhelming, it won't after you read about the temple!

▶ Research the life of George Müller. If you're short on time, you can cheat and go to the Internet. The man helped thousands of orphans on God's provision alone.

▶ Visit Crown Financial Ministries' webpage: crown.org. This ministry will knock your socks off. If ever there was a group of people dedicated to funding God's will, this is it. They understand that God asks us to do huge things, and then He provides the resources. They have Internet radio programs, books, calculators, articles . . . if you need it, they will have it.

▶ Check out *Little House on the Prairie* and read it cover to cover. You will be astounded at the bravery, sacrifice, and spirit of invention that the early American pioneers exhibited. You may be tempted to sell your car and buy a wagon and horse.

▸ Research living conditions in China, Ethiopia, Honduras, Italy, and Russia. You may be surprised that even modern countries have perspectives on needs that are vastly different from the perspectives Americans have. Many areas are so limited in space that no one has four bathrooms. Imagine that!

▸ Pray specifically about the finances. If you are married, pray together.

Don't give up hope if your finances appear to be unmanageable. Maybe God is about to unleash those vast stores of wealth on your behalf. Maybe you need to scale back your vision to God's understanding of "needs." Perhaps God is waiting for your generosity to be sown so He can help you reap His generosity. Keep praying and thinking, and eventually the money will sync with the vision.

STUDY QUESTIONS

1. What is this going to cost you?
   a. Financially:
   b. Time and Energy Costs:
   c. Other Costs:

2. How much of this cost can you cover yourself? Can you rework the budget, get an extra job, or reallocate some resources?

3. How much of this cost can you reasonably expect your family and friends to cover for you? Are they willing to help in creative ways, and how?

4. What is the remaining shortfall? After you have done all you can and your friends and family have helped as much as possible, what will you still lack?

5. As you consider all you will lack and your heart thumps with terror and unease, read Mark 9:14–27. Then rewrite verses 23

and 24 in your own words and place them someplace you will see them each day.

6. What can you change (TV habits, reading materials, social events) so that your perspective on "enough" aligns with God's?

7. Please look up the following verses and use them as encouragement for the financial side of your adventure:

   a. Matthew 6:25–34
   b. Mark 6:30–44
   c. Acts 4:32–35
   d. Ephesians 3:17–21

Maggie and Her Family Move around the World to Be Missionaries

During her college years, Maggie returned from a short-term missions trip determined that a missions lifestyle was what God wanted for her. She married a few years later, and her husband Dewayne shared her passion for missions. From the beginning of their marriage they planned to move to Central Asia as soon as possible, but actually getting to the mission field was full of delays and waiting. While they waited they could have given up. Instead, they made each new decision in light of what they knew God wanted them to do . . . eventually. Here's how Maggie described her situation:

The best physical example I can give was my vacuum cleaner. My mother bought us a Kenmore upright vacuum cleaner as a wedding gift. I believe she spent a hundred dollars for it. Thirteen years later it was being held together with duct tape, and the cord was wrapped in electrical tape so it didn't shock me. I could never justify getting a new one, though, because I always thought we would be moving overseas at any time. We made certain life choices based on living overseas. We chose to homeschool our kids from the beginning because we knew that's what we would do overseas.

One day at a ladies' Bible study we were supposed to share something we were thankful for. That day I was thankful for the fact that God had never taken away my desire to serve Him overseas. It would seem natural that with all the disappointments we faced I could have just thrown in the towel and said, "Okay, God changed His mind." But in my heart the desire resided, and I began to realize my original understanding was there, but the obedience was lacking.

I ended up writing down my thoughts and feelings and sharing them with my husband. He didn't come to the exact same conclusion, but he saw merit in what I was suggesting. I felt we had to give moving overseas one more chance, and if God absolutely refused us this time, then I would buy a new vacuum cleaner.

We spoke with the board of directors overseeing our campus ministry, and they gave us the green light to explore heading overseas. Thanks to the help of several friends, Americans and non-Americans, we were living in Central Asia within six months.

The family (Maggie and Dewayne have three sons) settled in Asia and attacked the first order of business: learning the language and starting new relationships. I know we would all like to hear that life is now smooth and easy, but here's the truth:

We've had to make some lifestyle choices. We don't own a car here. When we left the States, we sold our Honda Civic, which we had had for about six years. That same car would have cost twice as much here as what we originally paid. Gasoline is three times as expensive here as in the States. I won't even go into the driving practices! Living overseas comes with enough natural stress; we don't need to add to it exponentially. The public transportation isn't exactly reliable, but when you get lucky and don't have to wait too long, it's doable.

This does lead to another cultural stress, though. In this country I think it's safe to say 95 percent of the population smokes cigarettes, starting at about the age of fourteen. They also drink large quantities of black tea, all day long. So people hyped up on caffeine and nicotine are at times difficult to deal with. That isn't the main stress, though. The bad decision of smoking leads to hacking and coughing and rampant tuberculosis. Not all people on public transportation cover their mouths when coughing and sneezing. Or if they do, they proceed to use the hand they coughed in to grab the exit bar by the door. After one bus ride I usually feel like I need a shower. This has also led our family to being tested for TB. Thankfully, because of my husband's job we are able to use the socialized health care, and these tests are free.

Bringing three kids of varying ages overseas has been trying at times. I think it's safe to say we've run the gauntlet of emotions. One son had a very hard time with the initial transition but now doesn't want to leave. Another one was fine with coming and now he doesn't want to stay. I've had the same feelings at times. Unfortunately, for me, most days now feel like I'm serving a prison sentence. A variety of things feed into this feeling.

We constantly struggle with comparing life here to life in the States. The problem with our host country is that it *seems* so modern. There's an expectation that life here should be "easier" because of the modern feel, but because of the cultural way of thinking, that just isn't so.

We began learning language via the Rosetta Stone computer program before coming, and then we started using language schools once we got here. Both were helpful, but one day it dawned on me: I could learn this language to perfection, but not until I think like a local will I truly be able to understand them and communicate in a meaningful way. Not that the gospel couldn't be communicated adequately, but there is so much related to language from a cultural stance that any foreigner anywhere will ever only get so far.

Living overseas affects relationships from the States as well, both family and friends. Even with all the modern technology, "out of sight out of mind" rules the day. I really don't think anyone does this intentionally, but the American lifestyle is so fluid that if you're not there to hold a spot, it quickly gets filled or absorbed. Our first visit home was fine and people were very welcoming and seemed interested, but at the same time different. All you have to share are memories, and those only last so long. I had one sister cut all communication with me for one year because she felt we were putting our kids in harm's way. The relationship is on the mend, but it's still a matter of great stress.

Our situation is unique because we don't have a team to work with. This has its pros and cons, but one con would be lack of community. God has been very good to us and provided us with community repeatedly these past four years. One reason we chose to live in the city we did was because we knew it would have a large expatriate population (other Americans). This has proven true and provided for our various needs as individuals.

One continuous struggle here is finding balance to life. We have plenty of American friends now and plenty of ministry opportunities, but finding the balance of those things among work, homeschooling, and regular life is extremely difficult.

These struggles have taught lessons that Maggie will take with her into the future God has planned. Here's what she has to say:

I don't know what our future holds, but I do feel more prepared for a variety of things in life now. If we go back to ministry in the States, I feel I will be a better servant there. I can better relate now to being a stranger in a foreign land. I can better encourage the younger generations to go as soon as possible and start learning the language while their brains are fresh and ready. I can better empathize with the worker who is home visiting and feeling like they no longer belong anywhere.

If I could do it all over again I would, but I would have done it differently. Instead of getting married first, I think I would have spent a year or so as a single in the country. Paul is right about the gift of singleness (1 Corinthians 7). Having a family makes serving much more difficult.

But what about the vacuum, Maggie? Did you get a new one in Asia?

I've had to buy two! Things here can be junk. Thankfully, the weekly market has vacuum parts, so I'm starting to upgrade my latest one.

Our house in the States only has one small room with carpeting. If we return to the US and live in that house, I'm going to rip out the carpet. Then I won't need a vacuum anymore! ■

CHAPTER 7

Sacrificing Yourself

COLOSSIANS 3:1–4

Since, then, you have been raised with Christ, set your hearts on things above, where Christ is seated at the right hand of God. Set your minds on things above, not on earthly things. For you died, and your life is now hidden with Christ in God. When Christ, who is your life, appears, then you also will appear with him in glory.

Accomplishing the will of God is impossible without personal sacrifice. Personally, if it were up to me, I'd live on a tropical beach. I'd have a small mansion filled with beautiful and funky furniture. I'd have a doctorate in some interesting subject like Italian history, but my job would be to work in a library in the mornings. I'd spend my afternoons napping on the beach and my evenings out at fabulous restaurants with my husband and friends. I'd have children, of course, but the nanny would always be around waiting for me to need a break.

Let me assure you that this is not what God has called me to do. We live in Michigan, which is cloudy much of the year and frozen for four months solid. Our house is not a mansion nor is it near the beach. The furniture certainly is funky, thanks to Great-Aunt Helen and her 1960s castoffs. The nanny has yet to show up!

Most days my life is nothing but sacrifice for the people I love. I'm not complaining; it's the way it's supposed to be. The Christian life is about sacrificing what we want now for something much better later. Pleasing God now means giving up our natural desires. Not that this is easy. It's not. Often, it's not much fun either.

Whenever I think of sacrifice, I think of parenting. Biblically speaking, who were the number one parents? Mary and Joseph, of course. Talk about a job! The Christmas card industry shows cozy stable scenes where Mary and Joseph lovingly gaze at the baby Messiah. The angels are right outside the door singing beautiful music, and the shepherds are worshiping. Everything is peaceful and wonderful.

They do not show Mary's mother in the background freaking out because her precious daughter was having a baby out of wedlock.

They do not show Joseph's friends at the tavern next door, talking about how Mary got pregnant a bit early, and how it seems possible that Mary might be sneaking around behind Joseph's back.

They do not show Mary's friends walking down the other side of the street to avoid her in town, or giggling nastily as they pass her house.

No one ever thinks of how hard it must have been to parent Jesus. Have you ever spent much time with a kid you know is way smarter than you are? That child is always pointing out mistakes you've made, asking you questions you can't answer, and generally living in another dimension. I'm sure Jesus wasn't a horrible kid to parent, but I wouldn't be surprised if Mary and Joseph usually felt one step behind and a little bit dim.

When Jesus became an adult, Mary even had to sacrifice the usual expectations of adult children. I'm sure she would have loved to watch Jesus pick a nice Jewish girl and have lots of happy, pudgy babies, but His call was to wander around the countryside: poor, overworked, hated by the Pharisees, with no woman by his side. No babies to snuggle. No mother wants to see her child lonely, poor, or tired, no matter how old the child may be.

Finally, we cannot forget how Mary must have felt watching Jesus on the cross, knowing that her precious child was being treated like a criminal—since that was part of the plan for the entire world. God had a plan, she had a part to play in it, but she had no influence in the final outcome. Talk about sacrifice!

Parenting Jesus required that Mary and Joseph had to set their minds on things above and work for a higher calling. They had to ignore cultural expectations and family traditions, and I'm sure they lost some friends along the way. It must have been ostracizing to be known as the mother of the man who was crucified next to the thief. No good Jewish mother would have raised a child the religious leaders wanted dead.

God calls us to that level of sacrifice. We may be blessed with a relatively normal life, but we need to be prepared to give it up in a second and focus on blessings that only exist outside earthly reality.

"Comfy-Cozy" Is Not a Biblical Ideal

We love to be comfortable. Name any invention in your house, and I bet it ties into comfort somehow. Our dishes get washed without our hands being involved; our clothes get tumbled clean and freshened in metal boxes. Our microwaves get our food ready so quickly that we barely have time to get hungry. Our couches, chairs, and beds are squishy, covered in soft fabric, and ready for us to relax. Our floors are covered in carpet, and our furnaces are ready to keep the chill away. We love to be comfy. From where I type I can see my couch, I can see the fuzzy blanket, and I can hear them both calling to me. "Nap, Jessie. It's time for your nap . . ." Oh, how I love my cozy naps.

This, however, is not what God has called us to do all day. God offers us rest. He offers us peace. He offers us everything we need, but He is not hoping we'll settle into squishy insulated boxes and sleep until we die. He's called us to get up, find the people who need Him, and make sure things get done. People need to hear about Jesus; we need to tell them. People are hungry; we need to feed them. Children are born; we need to raise them. Students are ignorant; we need to teach them. Neighbors are lonely; we need to befriend them.

))) **God offers us rest. He offers us peace. He offers us everything we need, but He is not hoping we'll settle into squishy insulated boxes and sleep until we die.**

Mind you, there's nothing wrong with having a comfortable couch. But there is something wrong when the left-hand cushion has a permanent indent of your butt. Unless, of course, you have no working legs, and then I apologize profusely. You may sit and accomplish God's will. But you are the exception. The rest of us need to get up and get going.

I Used to Have Plans for My Future around Here Somewhere

Some of us are standing at a fork in the proverbial road, knowing that two destinations are beckoning. The left-hand path leads to the dreams *you* have for your future: becoming a doctor, traveling around the world, getting married, and having six kids . . . whatever you want.

However, the Lord himself is standing down the right-hand side, calling your name. You know that when you take one step toward Him you are taking a huge step away from what you have been hoping and planning for. Some of us have been working steadily toward a goal for years and years. Can we give it up?

I'm not going to lie—the prospect can be terrifying. God knows this! He understands that He is asking you to do something you never dreamed, wanted, or hoped to do. Talk to Him about it. Pray for peace, and take the first step toward Him. As you begin taking the steps needed to accomplish His plan, you'll notice that your old dreams seem far away and fuzzy. Soon they'll be nothing but memories from another time.

Do you remember the Christmas when you were eight years old? What did you want? Eight-year-olds take the business of Christmas seriously. They have the ability to plan, compare notes with other eight-year-olds, and beg incessantly. They are pretty sure life will end if they don't get what they want. What if someone walked up to you this Christmas and handed you the same thing you wanted so badly when you were eight? You'd be a bit flummoxed. "Gee, thanks for the My Little Pony Stable. I have a place for that right over on my china cabinet next to my good dishes. Or somewhere."

As you choose God's plan for your life, the dreams you used to have will be as important to you as the My Little Pony set. Because you grow and change and continually soak up God's presence into your soul, your mind-set will begin to reflect the things of God. In Romans 12:1–2, Paul says to the believers: "Offer your bodies as a living sacrifice, holy and pleasing to God—this is your true and proper worship. Do not conform to the pattern of this world, but be transformed by the renewing of your mind. Then you will be able to test and approve what God's will is—his good, pleasing and perfect will."

God's dreams can only become our dreams if we have transformed minds, which means we must be willing to release our own plans. There is no fence-sitting on this one, folks. We create misery for ourselves if we halfheartedly try God's plan while clutching at our own. It's possible that some of us are creating our own misery without even realizing it. Are we trying to please God and keep our own plans intact? Moving ahead with God often requires letting go of ourselves.

Two dear friends of mine each have sons with developmental delays. Let me assure you that when they held those precious babies in their arms, they did not anticipate the way life was going to turn out. Nothing came easily to those boys. Sleeping through the night took years. Walking was a year behind schedule. Social skills progressed, but at a painful, creeping pace. Each mother had to let her original dreams go and embrace the reality of God's plan for their family. The new reality is that they need to love their sons the way they need to be loved, not the way they had hoped to love them.

One of the boys, Jacob, is now in the fourth grade. With the help of a full-time aide, he's doing very well. His parents' hard, hard, *hard* work is paying off in its own time. God's reward for them will be tremendous! God's reward is tremendous for anyone who lets go of her own stuff to obey Him. Jesus taught His disciples this:

> "Whoever wants to be my disciple must deny themselves and take up their cross and follow me. For whoever wants to save their life will lose it, but whoever loses their life for me will find it. What good will it be for someone to gain the whole world, yet forfeit their soul? Or what can anyone give in exchange for their soul? For the Son of Man is going to come in his Father's glory with his angels, and then he will reward each person according to what they have done." (Matthew 16:24–27)

These two sets of parents have put endless hours into raising their sons. When the other little boy, Micah, was four, I spotted him sitting at a table and playing with all the other kids. The sight was so normal and ordinary that I almost missed the beauty of it. *He was sitting and playing with the other children.* His parents spent four years working like crazy, and their hard work was showing fruit. But the temporary, earthly fruit of a child playing with his friends is nothing compared to the rewards they'll receive in eternity. Can you imagine those enormous crowns that Jesus will hand them for their earthly service? James 1:12 says, "Blessed is the one who perseveres under trial because, having stood the test, that person will receive the crown of life that the Lord has promised to those who love him." If the size of the crown is based on the amount of sacrificial perseverance, these parents are going to need a wheelbarrow to cart the thing back to their heavenly mansions.

I Think I Want His Assignment, Lord

I admire Jacob's and Micah's parents because I don't think I could do it. Really, I barely manage to raise my own two children without emotionally scarring them from day to day; I'm pretty sure I'd be a failure at special-needs parenting. I look at the responsibilities those parents carry, and I know I couldn't do what they do.

But I know other people who have calls from the Lord that seem pretty excellent. Mentally I tell God, "Those assignments seem like exactly my cup of tea, Lord, so why don't you just let me at it? I want to be an author just like her! I want to have a best-selling book that brings readers to tears one minute and laughter the next. I'd like to earn so much money at this calling that I can build wells for entire chunks of Africa, Lord. *Why don't you bless me like you've blessed her, Father?*" (Can you imagine the anxiety and whininess God has to put up with from me?)

As I've learned more and more about the modern approach to writing, I've learned a terrible little trick. It's pretty easy to keep track of other writers' success, at least from a numbers and marketing standpoint. I can go to Amazon.com and see the current ranking of any book they have in the system. I can see when Ann

Voskamp or Lysa TerKeurst is selling a book by the buckets. I can check Beth Moore's Twitter account and see how many followers she has.* It's never a reassuring number, my friend. These ladies have more people comment on a single Facebook post within minutes than most people have all week! The angst this develops in me has taught me a lesson, so I don't check these numbers on purpose anymore. But sometimes I can't help but notice how well they're doing.

We're not just called to make sacrifices as we follow God; we often need to sacrifice our expectations of what God will do with our efforts. Contentment with our own calling from God can be a messy business. Of course we want to do well, and we want to see fruit for our efforts. We want to know that all this sacrifice is paying off, somehow. Comparing our mediocre success to the wild success of others can make our work seem useless and wasted. It makes us wonder if we're doing the right thing at all! Does God really want me doing this?

Or maybe we aren't comparing apples to apples. Maybe we are stuck comparing apples to oranges because someone we know has an entirely different calling, and it looks so much easier than the load God gave us. There are days I want to give up writing altogether and just go do something concrete. Something where someone tells me what to do, I do it, and we're all happy.

My husband spends his days making complicated doodads and gizmos for the transportation industry. He has a set of detailed instructions to follow exactly as he builds the parts and then he tests those doodads to make sure they are exactly to specifications. He passes them on to the shipping department and moves on to the next assignment. There's no guessing, no wondering if he should try this or that on social media, no agonizing over

---

* Beth Moore currently has over 453,000 Twitter followers. By the time you read this, she'll probably have a billion.

sentence structure or chapter headings. And on top of all this, he earns a living wage and gets three weeks of vacation every year.

Sign me up, Bob. I totally want that kind of calling from God. But here's the thing—God has given Eric the full-time job with the steady income because someone needs to pay the light bill in this house. The other one of us can be the crackpot who wanders around with a book in her hand, extolling the virtues of Pinterest as a valid ministry tool. (True story.)

In her book *Unglued*, Lysa TerKeurst discusses this very problem. She says that she challenges herself with this truth when jealousy attacks: "'I'm not equipped to handle what she has, both good and bad—and what she has is always a package deal of both.' In other words, I've been assigned a load I can handle."[1] Such truth! We see the good sides of other lives and callings, but we might forget the sacrifices these people make too.

Every morning my husband hauls himself out of bed at 5:00 so he can get to his doodads and gizmos. I stay in bed for a few more minutes, snoozing away. He spends the day with bosses and expectations, while the cat and I wander around the house eating brownies when we feel like it and maybe taking the day off to go shopping. (Me, not the cat. The cat hates shopping.) My calling demands that I spend a lot of time reading the Bible and praying, and *how great is that?!* Eric's job demands that he reads the instructions right so he doesn't destroy a $10,000 gizmo. I'll take the Bible over federal regulations any day, now that I think of it.

The Bible teaches that we're all important, and God has designed each of us with a special gift and a special responsibility to the body of Christ. Paul says:

> Just as a body, though one, has many parts, but all its many parts form one body, so it is with Christ. . . . If the foot should say, "Because I am not a hand, I do not belong to the body," it would not for that reason stop

being part of the body. . . . If the whole body were an eye, where would the sense of hearing be? If the whole body were an ear, where would the sense of smell be? But in fact God has placed the parts in the body, every one of them, just as he wanted them to be. If they were all one part, where would the body be? As it is, there are many parts, but one body. . . . Now you are the body of Christ, and each one of you is a part of it. (1 Corinthians 12:12, 15, 17–20, 27)

So, if you're an ear, be an ear and be it proudly! Be the foot if you're called to be a foot. You have a special design for just that purpose, and none of the other parts can do what you're designed to do. And stop checking Ann Voskamp's rankings on Amazon; the woman is a best-selling author, and that's just the way it's going to be. (Sometimes I need to sneak little sermons into the book just for myself.)

The Heart Sacrifices Are the Hardest

Way back in the first chapters of this book we talked about how sometimes God calls us to really big assignments, like Moses and the trek through the desert. Or maybe like that friend of yours who just left for Russia to be a missionary. But there are others of us who are called to much quieter, more personal things. Callings that affect our hearts, not our zip codes.

The same is true for sacrifices. Some of us have to make big, loud sacrifices that everyone can see. Things like giving up houses or good jobs or plans for the future. The sacrifice might not be easy, but at least it gives everyone something to talk about. "Did you hear about Sam? He's giving up medical school to go to Haiti. Can you imagine?" Sam's the hottest thing going at the family reunion, as everyone spreads his news from great-aunt to third cousin.

Some of us just have a lot of work to do on the inside, and no one will know but God and us. Our heart is a complicated thing. We get ideas stuck in there, we get opinions lodged in deep, and we hide away hurts. There's a certain way we want to live, a certain attitude we'd like to nurture, and it's often here that the Holy Spirit begins His work. If you think it's hard to sell your beloved house and move across the state, you should try a heart sacrifice. Now that's *hard*.

We are called to sacrifice our own ideas and opinions and choose God's opinions and ideas. That's really hard to do, because our attitudes are often based on pretty sound reasoning and we're hard-pressed to give them up. For example, I have a friend whose husband had an affair a few years ago. The marriage was beyond repair, and Cassandra moved out while the mistress moved in. Her husband was the one with the good income, so he kept the house while Cassandra moved into a mobile home park and worked for slightly more than minimum wage. She was soon saddled with legal bills she couldn't afford to pay for a divorce she didn't want, while sharing custody of her children with a woman who destroyed her family.

Really, do we blame Cassandra for her animosity toward her ex-husband? We would understand if she was tempted to run him over with the car. Heck, I've been tempted to nudge him a little with the Buick a few times, just for her sake. This is where the heart sacrifice gets costly. We want so much to hang on to our own attitude, but God says this is not the way to handle the situation. Jesus said, "You have heard that our ancestors were told, 'You must not murder. If you commit murder, you are subject to judgment.' But I say, if you are even angry with someone, you are subject to judgment! If you call someone an idiot, you are in danger of being brought before the court. And if you curse someone, you are in danger of the fires of hell" (Matthew 5:21–22 NLT).

Well. The fires of hell, huh? Serious business.

We've been called to a higher standard by the one who sacrificed everything for us. Ephesians 4:31–32 tells us to "Get rid of all bitterness, rage and anger, brawling and slander, along with every form of malice. Be kind and compassionate to one another, forgiving each other, just as in Christ God forgave you." That's what I mean when I say heart sacrifice. We naturally hold on to our bitterness and anger. Some of us might even love to brawl, I don't know. But when we're instructed to give up those natural reactions and choose kindness and compassion instead, that's a steep sacrifice. One we can manage only with the Holy Spirit's help.

It can be tempting to skip this step and just ignore these quiet sacrifices. After all, if no one knows but us, how important can they be? But I have to remind myself that Jesus spent His entire earthly ministry focusing on what happened inside a person's heart, not on outward appearances. These things might seem small to us, but they are huge on God's scale. And that's the only scale that matters, in the end.

Quiet, Meek, Everyday Heroes

I have yet to see anyone truly interesting on the cover of those magazines in the checkout lane. They show a lot of cleavage and shiny dresses and handsome men, but no real heroes. I want to see my step-grandmother on the cover of *Vogue*. The woman raised eight children, and when her first husband died, she married my stubborn (but sweet) ox of a grandfather. She then proceeded to put up with my extended family for twenty-five years, all of us as stubborn and ox-like as our grandfather.

As a family, we Morgans do not sing Christmas carols. We do not play Skip-Bo. We do not hug. All of Freda's biological family finds these activities perfectly normal, and even enjoyable. A regular woman would have given up hope in 1989 and shouted, "Fine! You are on your own, you grumpy and unpleasant people!" But not Freda. She has never given up on loving us, even when I'm sure a few times she would have liked to stick us with her meat fork instead of cooking us Thanksgiving dinner. I love you, Grandma. Thanks for loving us like Jesus would have, instead of poisoning us like we may have deserved.

I'd like to see my friend Deb on the front of *Good Housekeeping*. Deb is known as the "Kitchen Lady" at church because she is always in the kitchen. Always. Thanksgiving dinner at church? Deb is cooking. Sunday school snacks? Deb. You'll find her in the kitchen. She's there early; she stays late. She cleans, cooks, then cleans some more. She digs up snacks for me and all the other gluten-intolerant folks in the congregation. She has never once beaten a teenager that I know of, even when they leave the kitchen sticky and stinky. Her servant's heart is part of her call from God, and she has never walked up to the front of church and said, "I'm here for my applause and thanks. You may proceed with the adoration." One day far in the future Deb will pass away, and I shudder to think of who will arrange her funeral luncheon. We'll all be in the kitchen, lost and weeping. No one will know where the aluminum foil is. Deb, however, will be doing a jig in heaven, never to wipe up chocolate syrup again.

All I'm saying is that when we're obeying God, we have to sacrifice the desire for worldly applause and worship. That's for celebrities who are getting their fifteen minutes of fame and fortune right here on earth. It's as fleeting as the dew on the grass or the frost on my car. Freda and Deb, however, are working for thanks from a God who never forgets. He's storing up their blessings in heaven, one harassed Thanksgiving and messy kitchen at a time.

STUDY QUESTIONS

1. What is the sacrifice you fear the most? Do you think it might be part of God's plan for your life?

2. What comforts are most important to you? Do you think you can keep them and still wholeheartedly obey God? (For example, I do not think God is calling me to any ministry that does not include coffee. He does not want me killing people.)

3. What sacrifices can you imagine giving up easily?

4. Think of a friend who has made peace with a difficult life circumstance. How has that challenge enriched his or her life, as well as the lives around them?

5. Think of an everyday hero you know personally. What has he or she contributed to the people close by? What sacrifices has that person made?

6. Please read the following verses and consider the sacrifices you may be called to make:
   a. James 4:7–10
   b. 1 Peter 1:3–9
   c. 1 Peter 2:11–12

Anthony Gives Away His Watch

I'd like to introduce you to Anthony, fellow blogger and preacher from just below the Mason-Dixon Line. Here's a story about when he listened to God.

Let me tell you about a time when I felt . . . no, *I knew* . . . God was telling me, Anthony, to give my favorite new watch to a fellow preacher with whom I attended Bible school.

He was an older man, very simple and very humble. I was young and cocky, and I had a thing for nice watches. One night in class I noticed his watch's face was broken, and I heard a still small voice tell me, "Give him your watch." I tried to convince myself God was NOT speaking to me. To prove this, I knew God would never tell me to give away a gift. When somebody gives you something, you don't give the gift away, especially when it's from your wife. I felt I would surely get confirmation from my wife that I was simply feeling sorry for the guy, not hearing from God. I knew my wife would say something like, "Don't you dare give that watch away!"

No, she said, "You do whatever God tells you to do. I'm okay with it." *DANG IT!* So much for my excuse!

After a couple of weeks, I finally went up to my fellow minister and stood over him as he sat at a table in the classroom. I said, "I want to tell you that I am not particularly happy about what I am about to do, but I have to obey God. I like nice watches, and this is my favorite, but I noticed yours was cracked—God told me to give you mine . . . So here, I hope you like it."

Believe it or not (and you don't have to), all the negative feelings of giving my favorite watch away disappeared once I obeyed the Lord. And when I saw that humble preacher shed tears, it was worth it all. ■

CHAPTER 8

Overcoming Ignorance

PROVERBS 21:16

Whoever strays from the path of prudence comes to rest in the company of the dead.

PROVERBS 19:2

Desire without knowledge is not good—how much more will hasty feet miss the way!

Let's face it, many times God calls us to an assignment that doesn't require rocket science or an advanced degree or even a super brain. If God is asking you to befriend the elderly lady next door, all you need is a rake or a casserole, and you're in business. You march across the property line and smile. You spend a few hours raking or baking or listening, and you've made a friend. You then continue to look out for your neighbor and take her to the doctor and paint her trim and put up her Christmas lights. None of this requires any more than a willing heart and sensitivity to what she needs. God is pleased and everyone is richer because you stepped out in faith.

There are times, however, when God calls us to do something, and we realize we're in *way* over our heads. *What do I do? How do I do it? I am not equipped! In fact, I am so poorly equipped that I don't even know how bad it is yet!* Anyone who has ever brought a newborn home from the hospital knows exactly what I'm talking about. The sheer lack of knowledge is enough to make you want to call "Uncle!" and stop the game. Newborns turn funny colors, and they have flaps of skin that maybe shouldn't flap, and they make a lot of noise. And who knows how bad tomorrow will be? How will we keep this child alive tomorrow?

Apparently it doesn't end with infancy. Recently we ran into a friend we hadn't seen in several years. Marty's children are now older teens and college students, and he looked my husband and me in the eye, shook his head, and in an exhausted voice muttered, "You have no idea of what's coming. No idea." It's obvious that his children's adolescence has turned him into an old, broken man. Also a broke man. When we pressed him for details on how to prepare for our own children's teen years, he shook his head again and told us to make more money. *"They just cost so much money . . ."* he started. But then we were interrupted, and we never learned any more. We understand that we don't know anything, but it's coming for us anyway.

Second Chronicles 1 addresses this issue. King David had died, and it was Solomon's turn to run the kingdom. Solomon had offered a thousand burnt offerings on the bronze altar before the Lord in the Tent of Meeting, and that night God was pleased and appeared to him. "Ask for whatever you want me to give you," God said to him (v. 7).

What an opportunity! How many of us have dreamed of a moment like this, a moment to ask for whatever we want with the assurance that we'll get it? What would you ask for? How would you ask for it? Let's say that you were Solomon, with all the accreditations he had—the son of a king who happened to be one of God's favorite people *and* a future builder of God's house. If I were Solomon, I think I might have gotten just a tad bit cocky when the Almighty appeared to me. I might have preened a little bit, assuming that I must be quite impressive, if even God was noting my excellence. I probably would have stood a little straighter and held my nose slightly aloft, in a regal fashion.

But no. This is not how it worked out for Solomon, because apparently Solomon wasn't a pompous ninny like I am. His humility gives me shivers. If ever there was an excuse to get a big head, this was the time. But instead, Solomon recognized his need for wisdom so he could do a good job of being king. He said, "Give me wisdom and knowledge, that I may lead this people, for who is able to govern this great people of yours?" (2 Chronicles 1:10).

This humility further confirmed that Solomon's heart pleased God, who granted his prayer and *then* blew out Solomon's treasury with every kind of wealth. It was his humility that helped him to understand that he understood nothing. He realized he had no ability to lead a kingdom well by himself, so he asked God for the insight he needed to do it.

We can learn well from his example, because many of us are about to get a call from God that goes far beyond the simple task of befriending the elderly lady next door. We're about to get assignments that don't include rakes or casseroles or putting up a string of Christmas lights. One of us might even get an assignment to lead a nation. Where are we going to learn what we need to handle this task?

The Starting Point to Educating Yourself

Solomon started where we all must start—with humility. Let's take one step back and realize that God has infinite wisdom, ability, and resources. Why on earth He includes us in His plans is beyond me; He could do it all so much faster and easier by himself.

Everyone knows that when you need to go to the grocery store to buy nutritious food while sticking to a budget, you do not take the children. They slow you down! They interfere, they ask for sugary cereal that costs four dollars a box, and they knock down three cartons of eggs while you're hunting for your coffee coupon. In this instance, we are the children; God has taken us shopping anyway. This should humble every single one of us.

I don't really understand why God takes us shopping or involves us in any of His plans. Frankly, I do anything I can to go grocery shopping *without* my children. I will strategically map out my menu plan for days to avoid taking them to the store. "Let's see. If we have only potato chips and rice for dinner three nights in a row, I can wait to go grocery shopping until Monday morning when they are back in school. Yes, yes, and spaghetti sauce for breakfast every morning. Problem solved!"

So why, then, doesn't God do this to us? I know we must be as difficult as a child in a cereal aisle. Why does He seek us out, ask us to join Him, and patiently put up with our antics while we attempt to derail His plans through our own ignorance and misunderstanding? I have no answer for that. I only have the repeated experience of God asking me to join Him on a project. If I goof it up, He fixes it. If I run away, He comes after me. If I refuse, He stands there and taps His foot gently while I get my attitude in the right place. Sometimes He waits for years.

I think it must have something to do with love. Unending, unfathomable love from a Father to a child. Could it be that He loves us so much that just being with us, watching us grow, building a relationship with us is enough? Enough to cover the multitude of times we try His patience or goof up the plan when we act out of ignorance?

))) **Could it be that He loves us so much that just being with us, watching us grow, building a relationship with us is enough?**

That love humbles me and brings me right back to my need for wisdom. If I can't even understand why God would want to include me in this calling, how can I possibly understand what He needs me to do? I can't! But I can certainly ask my loving Father for what I need, and I can be assured, just as Solomon was, that He will make sure every resource I need is at my disposal. In Matthew 6:33, Jesus reminded us to "seek first his kingdom and his righteousness, and all these things will be given to you as well." We tend to think that God only gives us material or financial resources, but I strongly believe He gives us wisdom when we need it. Why else would James 1:5 tell us that "if any of you lacks wisdom, you should ask God, who gives generously to all without finding fault, and it will be given to you"?

I believe that every successful calling starts right here: a child who understands she is loved and who is willing to ask humbly for some help, and a Father who is willing to give anything needed to spend time with His child. From here we can move forward to get the information we need to handle this task.

The Source of Wisdom

Now that we understand where to start, we need to find our next step. Because this is a Bible study, you probably won't be shocked when I tell you the next step is to read the Bible. Now, I can hear you muttering at me under your breath. "That's very spiritual, Jess. Nice. But I think God's asking me to quit my job to homeschool my children, and I'm pretty sure the Bible is thin on curriculum guides." Or perhaps—"Jess, if you'd like to guide me to the Bible passage that directly addresses starting an Internet-based ministry to teenagers, I'd dearly love to read it."

This is true, because the Bible isn't a great font of wisdom if you're looking for specifics on engineering or the definition of the word "trumpery."* It can be a trifle thin on details, especially

---

* *Trumpery* means "useless nonsense." As in, I'd like to hope readers don't throw this book across the room due to the trumpery I've included. Like this footnote . . .

for our modern world. However, it is the best possible place to start for any wisdom you may be lacking in completing God's plan. In fact, the Word might be packed with information you need. You'll only discover it if you take days or weeks to study everything the Bible has to say about your assignment. You'll find a wealth of subjects there: adoption, mission work, finances, friendship, marriage, family, careers . . . you name it. By the time you've prayed and studied, you'll have a great understanding of God's heart on your subject. You'll be set to move on to the next step, whatever God may want that to be.

If you combine biblical wisdom with prayer, you have yourself an explosive combination. Step back, baby, things are about to get interesting.

Research and Study

Once you have a firm understanding of God's general view on the subject, you will need to dive into some specifics. This will, in fact, likely require that you look outside the Word of God. When some friends of ours decided to adopt, they had what seemed like three thousand choices. It took a lot of study into many different aspects of adoption: international or domestic? Babies or older kids? How many children? How much does it cost? Who would fit best with their biological children?

Research was necessary to make an educated decision, along with a lot of prayer. You may need to read many books on your subject, take classes, or find an expert in your subject. Don't be afraid to ask around and make it known that you are interested in learning more about a particular topic. You'd be surprised at what people know and are willing to share. Throw it out there on Facebook and see what sort of responses you get. I've received some of the best advice by just discussing things over with friends. On the other hand . . .

Seeking the Counsel of Others

Of course, many of us have asked others for input, and then we've been terribly, terribly sorry. (Facebook sometimes causes as many problems as it solves, you know? In fact, sometimes I throw out a question, get a lot of responses I disagree with, and realize the only reason I asked was because I knew the answer in the first place but wanted to make sure.) You just never know what people are going to think or say. It all depends on the situation and the person you ask for advice.

I can think of several issues to consider when picking someone's brain:

▶ You need to pick a person who is grooving on the same wavelength as you and God. Do not walk up to your ultra-liberal agnostic brother-in-law and hope to get sound spiritual advice. The bigger and more complex the issue, the more mature the Christian might need to be.

▶ Do not assume that one person has the definitive answer. Pray for guidance about who could best advise you in your situation. You don't want to base your entire decision on one person, but asking fifty-three people is going to give you fifty-three answers. Choose carefully.

▶ Consider the counselor's personality and personal hang-ups before assigning "God's Truth" to his or her opinion. Everyone has issues that may affect that person's ability to give you sound advice. Sometimes these past experiences may be exactly what you need to hear, but other times it may be unhelpful in the extreme.

▶ Consider the counselor's personality in light of your

own personality and the assignment from God. I have witnessed some really weird decisions made because a person got a crazy idea in her head and then asked only one other person for advice, and that person had the exact same personality. Try to ask people for advice if they are mature, successful (as God defines success), and have a personality that *balances your own*. For example, if you suffer from impulsiveness and have a hard time recognizing the consequences of your actions, do not ask your equally impulsive friend for advice. You may want to ask your calm, dependable preacher if you should sell everything to start a bungee-jumping circus ministry. On the other hand, if you're the solid, dependable, never-take-a-risk type, maybe you *do* need to chat with a friend who's a little more flexible or willing to take risks.

Can I Take Some Time to Pray about This First?

I've touched on this subject quite a few times, but we need to focus again on prayer for a moment. I realize this chapter is about educating yourself so you can move ahead with God, and prayer isn't *exactly* a form of education. It's far more important than that. If we go back to our initial conversation about Solomon asking for wisdom, you notice that he was talking directly with God. There was intimate communication between the two of them. We need this same type of relationship with God as we go about doing His will, and thanks to the Holy Spirit, we are always able to have exactly that.

We can study the Bible and other resources only so much. We can ask for good advice from only so many people. There's going to come a time when we have to move beyond that input and actually put all our learning into practice, and that's when we need to make sure we are tightly connected to God through constant, mindful prayer. Without humbling checking in for the program, we're guaranteed to steer ourselves wrong somewhere. Yes, the Bible will show us God's heart on a general subject. Aunt Betty may have lived as a missionary for fifty years in India, and she might have some wise things to tell us. We can look up websites and talk to experts until we have no more energy left in our bodies, and we still won't have the direct, specific, step-after-step directions that God wants to give us.

Prayer is the only thing that will get us the moment-by-moment information we need. We must go to God and listen carefully to what He says if we have any hope of success in His project. These verses from Romans 8:26–28 sum up everything I'm trying to say:

> In the same way, the Spirit helps us in our weakness. We do not know what we ought to pray for, but the Spirit himself intercedes for us through wordless groans. And he who searches our hearts knows the mind of the Spirit, because the Spirit intercedes for God's people in accordance with the will of God. And we know that in all things God works for the good of those who love him, who have been called according to his purpose.

I don't know about you, but I don't want any part of this grand plan of God's unless He is there with me, every single minute. I have no business writing or raising children or being married on my own wisdom. Trust me, friends. We're looking at epic disasters if I do this on my own. I need the Holy Spirit interceding for me in accordance with God's will. I need God working for my good, because I know I've been called for His purposes, but I also know they are much, much higher than any purpose I could ever understand.

I need prayer. I need more communication directly with my heavenly Father. How about you? How much time have you spent in prayer over this matter? I beg of you—don't move forward until you've prayed for it thoroughly and listened for the answer.

It Turns Out I Know Nothing

Prideful people often assume they know everything. They often make bad choices based on their own understanding, which is exactly what we do not want to do. Wise people, humble people, assume that God knows more, and they dedicate themselves to learning everything He has to teach on the subject. And then, only then, do they research and ask people for advice. Then they cover everything in a blanket of prayer. Is it possible we'll still stumble and make mistakes? Absolutely. But I believe God will see our humble hearts and work miracles on our behalf when we seek His wisdom first.

STUDY QUESTIONS

1. How well educated are you when you specifically consider this project God has planned for you?

2. What do you need to learn before you are a semi-competent member of God's team?

3. Do you know any experts in this subject? Find them and interview them.

4. Do you know anyone who did this with disastrous consequences? Find her, interview her, and learn from her mistakes. But be nice about it . . . don't make her cry. Find someone who is willing to talk about it.

5. Have you committed to pray about this project fervently?

6. Take some time (hours or weeks) and study what the Bible says about your new plan. If you don't know where to start, find a

Bible with a concordance in the back. Look up as many words as you can think of about your subject, and go verse by verse. Use a notebook to write down individual verses and how they specifically relate to your situation.

Cheri Fields Starts a Blog on Creation Science

Cheri and I corresponded via our blogs for quite a while before we realized we live less than an hour from each other. Life's funny like that. What's also funny is that she felt God calling her to do something she wasn't ready for at all. I know just how she feels.

This isn't the first time God has called me. Back in my teens I visited Moscow, Russia. A few years later, I spent a week in the Czech Republic. So, when God introduced me to a guy heading to Germany as a long-term missionary, I said *yes* to God, the guy, and the call.

Six years later, I was feeling a bit desperate. Being in the ministry often means learning what being "poor as church mice" feels like, and the thing bothering me most was the lack of funds to send on to other ministries. Not to mention the inability to finance a lifelong desire to see the Holy Land for myself.

What could a homeschooling mom with a flock of Littles do to bring in funds?

Learn to write.

God provided the finances for that training, showing me He had no objection to my chosen path. I even found out through trial and error what kind of writing He'd gifted me in. It sure isn't novels! But I had so much fun writing nonfiction I wanted to do more. Lots more.

When I finished the writing course, I was ready to launch out. What should I focus on? My best work had been writing science for kids. It was always my favorite subject and something I had continued learning just for fun as an adult.

Then I realized it wouldn't be any fun talking about science without being able to say, "Isn't God amazing?" That put a big brake on for me. The world doesn't always treat people kindly who speak out for God as Creator. Surely there were lots of other people already putting out great stuff in the Creationist community. But God wouldn't let me look for a more comfortable area to write in.

I decided to see what was out there. To my surprise, delight, and horror, only a puny amount of info was being put out for kids. Even the most basic web address I could think of (creationscience4kids.com) was available at a rock-bottom price.

Maybe God was telling me something. But there was no way I wanted to stick my neck out where people who didn't agree with me were sure to give me a hard time. I'd heard what some people say about Creationists. The last thing I wanted was to debate people who hate my guts.

Two weeks into this quiet struggle, a magazine came from the Institute for Creation Research. On the Letters to the Editor page was a note from an eleven-year-old kid saying how much he appreciated their writings. Even though he couldn't understand a whole bunch of it.

I've been getting that magazine for years. From what I recall, that's the only time a kid has ever written the editor.

"Okay, God. I'll do it. Help me be strong when the attacks come," I prayed.

This isn't something people can understand unless they've experienced it, but I felt as if God was thrilled. I'd never felt anything like it before, even when I'd committed to serve in a foreign land for a lifetime.

The first year I ran my website, no one knew my name because I was scared. For a while, no one read anything I wrote, so there was no attack. Then God called me to get into social media. I know trolls bother more than just Creationists, but it was amazing how many of my early interactions consisted of communicating with contrary-minded people.

About six months into my ministry, I could no longer face turning on the computer each day. I knew there would be difficult things to deal with, and I was tired.

One night I talked to God about it, and a thought popped right up. I imagined sitting around in heaven trading "war stories." Some will share how they were thrown out of their homes, imprisoned, and laughed at. When it's my turn, I will be able to tell them how I had some of the brightest atheists throwing their best arguments at me. I'll say that I had to rely on God and His Word, but I never backed down. How great will that be?

This idea was revolutionary to me—I hadn't thought of it like that! Sure, I'm not being physically threatened, but this apologetics (a word I got to know fast that year) work does sound impressive!

I still don't enjoy facing off against people who oppose biblical teaching—as Paul did in Corinth (Acts 18:6), but it's never been as exhausting again either. My attitude toward it is completely different. Plus, I learned to set limits and to pray.

Now if someone comments on my page more than once, they go on my prayer list. Let the Holy Spirit do the work and bear the burden! I pray for my whole site too.

Before starting online, I couldn't give you the full name of a single person I knew who wanted nothing to do with Jesus. Now I have a handful, living around the world, I pray for daily. My site has reached into homes in practically every country, and many of those people live in places where the gospel is opposed by the government.

I'm still waiting for the financial side to make an appearance (that should be changing soon), but I've gotten to know and interact with a huge number of fellow believers, and I've received a number of review books I couldn't have afforded otherwise. Also, my kids are excited about writing, apologetics, and geography. I've experienced God's ability to work through everyday people in a whole new way. My confidence in the reality and power of God has moved beyond simple acknowledgment of principle to practical experience. ∎

CHAPTER 9

Planning Flexibility

ECCLESIASTES 3:1–8

There is a time for everything, and a season for every activity under the heavens: a time to be born and a time to die, a time to plant and a time to uproot, a time to kill and a time to heal, a time to tear down and a time to build, a time to weep and a time to laugh, a time to mourn and a time to dance, a time to scatter stones and a time to gather them, a time to embrace and a time to refrain from embracing, a time to search and a time to give up, a time to keep and a time to throw away, a time to tear and a time to mend, a time to be silent and a time to speak, a time to love and a time to hate, a time for war and a time for peace.

I know you have that old song "Turn, Turn, Turn" in your head now. You're humming it right now. I Googled it to see who wrote it, and it turns out that Pete Seeger wrote it in the late 1950s. I learned all of this from Wikipedia, which is currently the only way I learn anything useful. A few different bands recorded it, but I think the Byrds did the version that's ripping through your head. I apologize if you wake up in the middle of the night with it stuck in your head. I hate when that happens.

Anyway, on to the point: all those seasons of life require flexibility, and a life of following God requires more flexibility than most! God himself never changes, but our lives here on earth are never the same from day to day. Imagine that you are a river. Sometimes the water flows in a smooth, straight pattern. Then all of a sudden the current picks up, and it looks like you're careening for a line of trees. Suddenly, the water changes direction as you whip around a bend. Then, in the distance you see . . . nothing. The river ends. But it doesn't really end—it just drops two hundred feet because there's a waterfall. You free-fall and land in the lake at the bottom. But the current continues to move even though it appears the lake is still. You find yourself leaving the lake and moving on to a new section of the river. You can see only a small portion of the journey at any given time, but Someone up above can see the whole river at once and is directing it to the proper destination.

Rivers serve different purposes at different places. Some spots are great for fishing; others are shallow and easy for small children to play in. In some places the water rushes so strongly that we capture the energy to create electricity. Deep spots can be used to transport goods. Our lives are similar. Different times serve different purposes. Following God's plan means stepping back and considering the whole river at once, and not getting caught up in the tiny bends and quirks. We need to consider our lives as a whole and head toward the final destination.

If ever there is a biblical example of flexibility, it is the disciples. They were just normal men—until they were befriended by Jesus, drafted into a three-year ministry, shown the very power of God, blessed with the Holy Spirit, and handed their own ministries. I am pretty sure that every day held a new experience. I wonder if each disciple was naturally flexible, or if they had to fight their impulses for continuity and normalcy like I do. Did Andrew ever pass a fishing boat and resist the urge to run back to what he knew, to the family business where he felt comfortable and confident? Did the constant need for flexibility ever wear him thin?

Back when I was in high school and college, I worked in pharmacies for my pizza/book/gas money. To this day when I get a prescription filled I have to fight the urge to climb over the counter and start counting my own meds out. I want to answer the phone; I want to call Dr. Dickinson's office to check if Mrs. Smith can have a refill on her hormones or her antidepressants or both. There is a rhythm to working in a pharmacy, a rhythm you can depend on. There are days as a writer when I'd love to have that simple formula back—stand behind a counter, count out drugs, and chat with elderly people. My life now—the parenting, the church membership, the career—all require that I plan for each day to be totally different. *And I'm just not very good at that, okay?*

I'm hoping the disciples were a lot more flexible than I am. When Jesus called His first disciples, they were fishing. Matthew 4:18–20 says: "As Jesus was walking beside the Sea of Galilee, he saw two brothers, Simon called Peter and his brother Andrew. They were casting a net into the lake, for they were fishermen. 'Come, follow me,' Jesus said, 'and I will send you out to fish for people.' At once they left their nets and followed him." They worked with Jesus for three years, doing everything from preaching to healing to praying, to traveling to fishing . . . again.

At the end of Jesus' three-year ministry, the disciples knew that everything was about to change. They weren't certain what exactly the new plan would be, but it must have been obvious that *something* was about to happen. Jesus had been crucified and resurrected and had appeared to His followers. The disciples had no choice but to wait out the lag between the end of Jesus' ministry and the beginning of their own ministries.

Can we slow this scene down and try to imagine what it felt like to be one of Jesus' followers after His resurrection? The days of the crucifixion, burial, and resurrection brimmed with emotion and activity. Maybe the disciples spent those days coming up with Plans A, B, and C. "If this happens, then I'll do that. But if that other thing happens instead, then probably we should do something altogether different. On the other hand, maybe the soldiers will show up this afternoon and *kill us all*, so all this planning might be *useless*."

That's the ultimate definition of flexibility right there. If your plans for the afternoon might need to include your own assassination, and you're okay with that, then you are, indeed, flexible.

In the middle of all this emotion, Jesus kept popping in and out. He appeared. He disappeared. Back again, gone again (John 20:19–21:4). This would have driven me mad, if I may be blunt. My emotions, already maxed out on stress and sadness and joy, would have been flopping back and forth with wild abandon. I would have needed some serious forward motion, like Jesus appearing in the clouds and taking Rome by storm with a host of angels. Or I would have needed for Him to make some sort of bold and final proclamation, letting me go back to my peaceful old fishing village where I could die as an old, wrinkly fisherperson. I would have fallen at His feet begging for a plan for my own sanity's sake.

That's how I would have reacted, but what did the boys do while they waited? John 21:3 says, "'I'm going out to fish,' Simon Peter told them, and they said, 'We'll go with you.'" They returned to what they knew. They were flexible. Obviously Jesus had other things for them to do other than fish, but they didn't know exactly what that was. They had to wait a bit, and they managed to do it with grace and patience. Flexibility in action.

Do you think Jesus could have worked with them if they were stubborn and inflexible? I don't think so. Yes, they had trouble understanding what Jesus was doing on the earth and what His ministry was going to be about. They were expecting a political leader and freedom from Rome. But Jesus worked with them, taught them, and was patient with them. Eventually they started to see what following Jesus really meant and would really cost them, and they developed into some of the most passionate, Holy Spirit–filled ministers the world has ever known. But before any of that, they had flexible hearts.

Seasons of Life—Cutting Yourself Some Slack

Take a moment to reconsider our passage from Ecclesiastes at the beginning of the chapter. There are different seasons of life. Priorities change depending on the requirement of the moment. God understands that, and remember that He is looking at the big picture. If you are in a season of life that requires total care for another human being (babies or elderly parents come to mind), then that may be God's plan for your life right now. Don't worry if you aren't accomplishing some huge goal like translating the Bible into Norwegian.* In fifteen years you'll have enough time to yourself that you can focus on your translations, or great works of art, or whatever project God calls you to do.

When my babies were tiny, this concept totally escaped me. I had these small creatures who were completely dependent on me to keep them alive. It was a 24-7 job. I also felt that my house had to be clean, my dishes done, the bread baked from scratch, and the laundry always folded. I worked at church, volunteered in the nursery, and helped keep the church's finances straight. I was insane, and I don't know why I didn't just sit down and reorganize my priorities. A person can only do so many things at one time without becoming a zombie. I barely remember my kids' early months, and I think that mostly had to do with running around like a nut while only getting five hours of sleep each night in thirty-minute chunks. This wasn't God's plan for my life; it was me planning my own life. Trust me, it didn't work out too well. Learn from my mistake, and be at peace with the one project

* Alert! It turns out the Bible has already been translated into Norwegian. You can find something else to worry about.

God has given you right now—even when it seems like you're not doing enough. You are! You are doing enough, so do it well.

)))   **Ask yourself: Is this God's plan for my life, or my plan for my life?**

"Flex, Don't Freak"

We obviously need to make plans for the future. Just bumbling along through life only gets us bumbled. No one wants that. However, let's not get so sure of God's plan that we cast it in cement and find ourselves unable to move when He calls us to something different.

My friend Maggie has worked on the mission field in countries where missionaries are not welcome. One particular trip required her to find her own place to stay for the night and find a ride back to the mission's quarters, alone. Mind you, Maggie is a medium-sized white woman. You go wandering around the Middle East looking like that and you'd *better* have Jesus on your side. You'd also need a pretty flexible attitude. One of the things she learned over the years was the little mantra "Flex, don't freak." She taught me this, and I mutter it under my breath whenever life upsets my plan or schedule. As I grow older and less flexible, I mutter it a lot!

Take a deep breath, and remember that rivers always change directions. You've never seen a river run in a smooth, straight line to the sea, have you? No. They twist and turn, loop and switch. You've also never seen a river stop moving and give up. It always reaches its destination.

Go ahead and do your best to accomplish God's will at the present time. Just don't be surprised if everything is different next week. You may lose or change jobs, you may get pregnant, you may be in an accident (a different accident than getting pregnant). Don't freak out. God is still in control. You only need to do your best and adjust to the new circumstances.

Flexible Understanding of Ourselves

I was on the campus of Western Michigan University a few weeks ago, back in a place where I spent a great deal of time in my carefree youth. I watched all the students carefully, remembering those years when my whole life seemed like an unending possibility. I had no idea of what I was going to do with myself. I could get married and move ten miles away (which is what I did) or stay single and get a master's degree in Rome (which I did not do but sometimes wish I had. Except for the single part—I still would have married Eric, and he would have come with me to Rome).

Now that I'm in my thirties, I have a better understanding of who I am and who God needs me to be. The problem is that I tend to clamp down on one aspect of my life and then refuse to consider any other options. How do you define yourself? Are there many aspects to your life? Do you look forward to changing those definitions as the years pass?

If we only consider ourselves in a single aspect, we may miss an opportunity to serve God in an unexpected way. Remember Moses? The man went from prince to shepherd to leader of God's people. Remember Esther? She went from orphan to queen to protector of God's people. Remember David? He went from shepherd to soldier to king to adulterous king to forgiven king to temple designer. Our lives are fluid. College students know that, and we have to continue to remind ourselves as we get older and more set in our ways.

If you find yourself becoming more and more inflexible as you age, I recommend that you fight against it as hard as you can. I know it's uncomfortable—I am feeling the same discomfort.

I want everything to be the same day after day, with a limited amount of variety just for fun. Variety like this: Do I want the Cinnamon Chex this morning with cherry flavored coffee, or Vanilla Chex with the Seattle blend beans? That's my speed of variety. But if I keep this up, I'm going to be that little old lady who has three pairs of the same shoes, just in different colors. I'm going to drive the same route to the grocery store every day at 7:43, and I'm going to get mad when the mailman is more than fifteen minutes late.

How is God going to work with a heart set in concrete like that? I don't know! I wonder if He'd even try! Maybe He'll go find someone with a tender, flexible heart and let her have all the fun of working with Him. And we old grouches will sit in our houses where nothing ever changes, missing out on the wonder that comes with flexibility.

We Need a New Life Plan

There are times in every life when it appears that your river is ending. Kaput. You're looking ahead and seeing nothing. As we previously discussed, it's probably a waterfall, and you're about to get your life rearranged for you. This chaos is never pleasant, and usually it leaves us feeling disoriented and out of control.

Instead of freaking out, we are going to sit down and breathe in and out. Flex, don't freak. Flex, don't freak. Now, let's assess the situation and find a new plan.

- ▶ Where am I? Am I still near friends and family, or have I landed someplace new and unfamiliar? Do I need new friends or a new church?
- ▶ Who am I? Am I now a parent or grandparent? Do I have a new career? What am I supposed to do with myself? How do I serve God in this new role?

- ▸ What needs to be done? Are there things around me that need my attention?
- ▸ How am I going to do it? Think through all your options to get the job done. Think outside the box, because heaven knows your old box is useless.
- ▸ Why did this happen? Did your life get rearranged because God is directing you to a new place or because of something you've done? Are you content with the outcome? Talk to God about it; He'll give you wisdom if you ask for it.

There was a time, as I first started writing this book, when I was staring into my own future with the blank feeling we're discussing. I was freaked out. I had nine months before my son started all-day kindergarten. Mind you, I'm not one of those mothers who weeps on the first day of school. I'm the kind of mother who lovingly drops the child off and spends six hours at the mall, celebrating the whole day. I *love* school.

Be that as it may, I was about to have major free time for the first time in seven years. Monday through Friday, 7:30–3:00. What was I going to do with myself? It's easy to feel useful when children are small and require all that care, but I knew I wasn't going to feel useful if I spent one hour a day attending to household chores and five more watching TV. Also, the family budget was indicating that I should probably get a real job.

I'm glad to report that God was faithful! What appeared to be an end was just a bend in the river. God led me to the perfect part-time job at my kids' school, which gave us a little extra income and gave me time to write for two years. After those two years our situation changed again, and I quit my job to write and volunteer in the community. God led me to the next sections of my river when the times were right, and I know He can do the same for you!

STUDY QUESTIONS

1. "Come, follow Me!" Jesus is calling. What "nets" do you need to set down in order to follow Him?

2. When you start to panic, how do you calm yourself down?

3. Think of a friend who is flexible and adjusts easily. How do you think he or she does that? Do you have any of those skills? How can you get some if you don't have them already?

4. What do you plan to do if you have to wait a long time for God to accomplish His plan?

5. How do you define yourself? How will you redefine yourself into God's image of you?

6. Think this through honestly and prayerfully: Are you in a season of life right now that absolutely requires you to focus on one thing? How can you manage this time of life and God's long-range plan for your life without losing your mind or disobeying God?

7. Look up these passages of Scripture. Think about all the ways these people had to be flexible or change their lifestyles to follow God:

   a. Luke 1:5–25
   b. Luke 5:27–32
   c. John 21:1–14
   d. Acts 2:42–47

David's Family Adds a Baby While He's Still in University

Did you catch that little part in David's earlier story about how his wife became pregnant with their third child before he graduated from the University? Let me assure you that this deserves its own spot—it's a great story.

This follows on from the first situation. It was October 1987. I was one month into my final year as a mature student at University (I was thirty years old by now). Marilyn, my wife, wasn't well, and I was worried. She finally made an appointment with the family doctor one Friday afternoon. I had arrived home early from my weekly commute to/from Uni (seventy miles away in Cardiff), and I took Nick and Michael to the local swimming pool while Marilyn went to her appointment. When she met us at the pool, she was smiling. This made me think that she wasn't going to die. I asked her what the problem was, and she replied, "Don't you know?"

I am male—how was I supposed to know?

"I'm pregnant," she said. The illness had been all-day morning sickness! "We're having another baby. In May."

By now my mind was working overtime. "A baby—in May? What date in May?" The date Marilyn gave me was right slap bang in the middle of my final examinations. By now my mind was in meltdown, and the wrong things were coming out of my mouth. Things like:

"Why are you smiling?"
"How are we going to manage if you have to leave work?"
"That is right in the middle of my exams. I am going to fail!"
"How can we support another child?"
"What are we going to do?"

It did all calm down eventually. We had a rocky weekend. I was unprepared for the news that we were going to have another child. I went back to Uni and I started to pray. I prayed for the baby to be born two weeks early. And I prayed for the baby to be born two weeks late. And so I alternated with my requests/demands, not really knowing which one was best. Two weeks early would mean the birth was out of the way, and I would be able to get on with my exams. Two weeks late would mean that the exams would be over and I could relax.

Then one day God spoke crystal-clear to me in a way that only He can: "The baby can be born two weeks early or two weeks late, but why don't you let me make that choice for you?" This was somewhat humbling. After weeks, perhaps months, of me trying to decide what was best, I realized that I had never surrendered the problem to God, which is what I should have done in the first place.

So I did. I am not saying that I was brimming with confidence at this point, but I knew He could work things out better than I could. I still didn't understand why He'd had chosen to add to our family at such a critical point in our lives. Once I had this word from God, I still wasn't sure about letting Him make the decisions!

Some strange things happened along the way. I was living in a University house on a recently constructed campus in my third year. There were halls, a dining hall, and laundry facilities on this site, but it was accessible to the public. The public included the local louts who would come on-site and damage things, leave taps running in the laundry, and threaten students. Because I was older than all the other students, I was the one to confront them, chase them off, and go to a telephone call box and summon University security. Because of this, the University installed a telephone in our house. This was before the age of cell phones. Students did not have telephones in their houses, especially when the houses in question were owned by the University. This meant that Marilyn could call me, as she did on the morning that she went into labor.

The second thing that happened was that Marilyn found she could no longer fit in the driver's seat of our car, so she told me to use the car to go back and forth to Cardiff instead of using the train.

This meant that when the "I'm having this baby today" call came, I was on the road and home in about ninety minutes.

That call came at 8:30 on the day before my finals. It was a Thursday. On Friday morning I was scheduled to have a three-hour examination in Quantitative Methods (statistics). Since this involved a lot of mathematics, I figured I could get through it by leaving revision until the day before the exam and working through past papers from the last three years as my revision. All the other exams would mean essay writing, so I had prioritized revision for these papers.

I can't tell you what was going through my mind as I drove home! I think it went something like this: "What do you think you are playing at, God? I trusted you to pick the best day for the baby to be born. How is the day before my exams the best day? Don't you know I haven't done any revision for Quantitative Methods yet?" I forgot completely about praying for Marilyn, the baby, or the midwife.

I arrived home sometime after 10:00 (we had elected for a home delivery, which was unusual back then). Marilyn's mum was there along with our doctor, two midwives, and a couple of social workers who had some strange interest in being present during a home delivery! James was born at about 12:15. There wasn't a lot of space in our bedroom with so many people in attendance, but it was quite something. Three hours later I picked up Nick and Michael from school. I remember that Michael was upset that James was not female. I took them home and soon after that left my mother-in-law in charge and hit the road back to Cardiff where my questioning of God and His timing continued.

When I got back to my student house, I was exhausted (I had just had a baby),* so I went to bed and set the alarm for 4:00. When the alarm sounded, I got up and did the only thing left to me. Pray? No, I revised all my formulae for the Quantitative Methods exam.

When I got into the exam room, I breezed through the exam. I couldn't believe it. Then I drove back home, collected the boys from school, and we got used to being a family of five instead of four. I left my mother-in-law in charge again and went back to Cardiff

---

* Oh, you did, did you? YOU had the baby? —Jessie

on Sunday after church. I then resumed revision for my other five papers. I had exams Tuesday–Friday, then another weekend at home, returning to Cardiff again on Sunday. I had Monday free before my last paper on Tuesday. Then I went home for the rest of the week.

When I asked God again, He told me that the day He had chosen was the best day. It was also the only option I had never considered. If James had been born a couple of weeks early, I would never have been able to focus on my revision or my exams. If James had not been born before my exams, I would have had difficulty concentrating, as I would have been expecting news about the baby at any time.

The only day James could have been born was the day that he was born. God knew that. It was all written into His plan of my going to University in the first place. Today James is twenty-five, newly wed, and very actively involved in a church with a significant outreach to students, as is his wife.

I learned that hearing from God means listening for that quiet whisper instead of bombarding Him thoughtlessly with a series of demands or a prayer shopping list. When God spoke on this occasion, He didn't shout, but what He said brought me to a halt as I thought, "Why didn't I think of that!"

And that is the problem. What we want is not necessarily what He wants (and vice versa). But I also see God's sense of humour in this. And it is good to remember that He has one. ■

CHAPTER 10

Encouragement In, Encouragement Out

1 THESSALONIANS 5:11

Therefore encourage one another and build each other up, just as in fact you are doing.

Encouragement from others isn't *necessary* if we are going to follow God. We can do without it, probably. But who would want to? Encouragement can make the difference between years of slogging through a difficult chore or joyously completing a welcome activity. And where do we get this encouragement, this strength to power through the challenge? From other people who love us and understand!

It's not a one-sided desire, though. We love to be encouraged, but so does everyone else. We need to form a community of encouragement, each of us cheering on others to follow God to the best of our ability. So, quickly run off and find your cheerleading costume. Dig out the old pom-poms. Convince your friends to join us, because this is a group effort, my dears. Repeat after me:

Go, team!

Go, team!

We can do it,

Yes we can.

We can do it

Because God says we can!

Go, team!

(Possibly the worst cheer ever. Forgive me.)

Thanks for Your Support

Friends and family often play a key role in our ability to move to the next step in God's plan. If encouragers surround you, they're right there supporting you and moving you along. They help you refocus and try again when you fail. They offer kind words. They pray for you. They buy you special treats and take you out for dinner when you're broke. Whatever it takes to keep you on the job, they're willing to offer what you need.

If Negative Nellies surround you, your experience will be entirely different. The job will seem even more uncomfortable. Loneliness and self-doubt will plague you. You might wake up each morning and seriously consider quitting it all and running off to Bermuda to live in a beach hut. All of this can be avoided if we simply have the encouragement we need, and if we make sure we are working hard to give others what they need to succeed at the life God has given them.

Let's take a look at an ancient friendship that shows us just what encouragement can do. Or was it an ancient family? It's sort of a muddle, frankly. Ruth and Naomi were not blood-related, but they stuck together like they were. Naomi and her husband, Elimelech, had moved from Judah to Moab when a drought choked Judah. They had two sons, who eventually grew up and married two Moabite women, Ruth and Orpah.

Elimelech and his two sons died, leaving three grieving widows. This would still be an emotional crisis today, but it was a genuine all-around crisis back then. It wasn't like Naomi could take a few classes to renew her nursing license and get a good job at the local hospital. The protection and provision of a man was often the only thing that kept a woman out of poverty. Naomi determined that she had only one choice and that was to go back to her own people in Judah.

Ruth decided to go with her and would not be dissuaded.

Naomi tried to talk her into going back home to her parents, but Ruth responded: "Don't urge me to leave you or to turn back from you. Where you go I will go, and where you stay I will stay. Your people will be my people and your God my God. Where you die I will die, and there I will be buried. May the LORD deal with me, be it ever so severely, if even death separates you and me" (Ruth 1:16–17). From this short statement, we can conclude that Ruth was a stubborn lass, but a stubborn lass who was willing to go the course for someone she loved. Naomi might have gone home to Judah to die, but Ruth was okay with dying right next to her.

The two women journeyed home to Judah and found a place to live together. Ruth went out to the barley fields to gather some leftover grain so they didn't starve, soon attracting the attention of Boaz, the wealthy and kindhearted landowner. Naomi came up with a little plan to get Boaz thinking about how he could marry that cute, brave Ruth and start having lots of little, pudgy babies with her. The plan worked, Ruth and Boaz got married and had a baby, and the final scene of the book shows Naomi caring for the new baby, overjoyed at his birth.

Forgive me for summarizing a beautiful story in a few sentences, but I want to focus on where this story went right. These women, stuck in the middle of a gigantic crisis, could have turned on each other at any point. We're looking at a situation right out of a soap opera, aren't we? But where's the fighting? Where's the depression-induced self-pity that led either woman to scar the other with hopelessness or bitterness? You won't find it, because it didn't happen.

Yes, Naomi was deeply disappointed in how her life had turned out. In verses 1:20–21 she tells her family from Bethlehem, "Don't call me Naomi. . . . Call me Mara, because the Almighty has made my life very bitter. I went away full, but the

LORD has brought me back empty. Why call me Naomi? The LORD has afflicted me; the Almighty has brought misfortune upon me." She could have taken that pain and discouraged Ruth—sucked the hope right out of her. Ruth could have returned the favor by abandoning Naomi or making her life miserable in a hundred different ways.

They both could have given up and died on the side of the road to Bethlehem, two miserable women with no joy in the future. No one would have blamed them. But God rarely includes people in His Word who just shrivel up and die with no plan, no greater redemption involved. Ruth and Naomi were no different. God had plans for each of these women, and by sticking together and encouraging one another, they were able to see that plan fulfilled.

Contrast Naomi's sadness in the early days with her hope at the end. Her friends said to her, "Praise be to the LORD, who this day has not left you without a guardian-redeemer. May he become famous throughout Israel! He will renew your life and sustain you in your old age. For your daughter-in-law, who loves you and who is better to you than seven sons, has given him birth" (4:14–15). Then Naomi took the baby on her lap and cared for him. Her days were full, her future was secure, and she was loved.

This story goes beyond two women, Boaz, and a baby. They named the baby Obed, and he was one of King David's, and therefore Jesus', ancestors. Ruth and Naomi's friendship was the link that brought history together at a critical point.

Your friendship and encouragement may be the very link that brings two people together, changing history. Have you ever considered your own part in future world events? What are you doing right now that will ripple to generations past us?

When I first went to college, I attended Indiana Wesleyan University. I was happy there except for the fact that I had no major, and it was a pricey place to hang out without a discernible educational goal. I felt God calling me to transfer closer to home to Western Michigan University. (Officially, this was the first time I heard God asking me to do something I feared and wanted no part of.) I sucked it up, transferred, and stepped out in faith (also, terror). The only thing I knew about secular universities is that they are often filled with heathens (this is exactly like the real world, I know now). I felt certain I was going to be the only Christian on a campus of twenty thousand students.

Happily, I was not the only Christian, and I soon found a fantastic group of fellow believers at His House Christian Fellowship. I met Eric, the man whom I married and is now sitting three feet away from me while he reads a book. But also, my friend Sara came with me to His House. There Sara met Dayton and married him a few short years later. Sara and Dayton now have three children. I fully expect one of them to change the world someday, and I'm going to take all the credit. I'm going to hobble up to Molly at her presidential inauguration and say, "Your mother never would have met your father if I hadn't transferred universities back in 1996. Now give this old lady a kiss." Humble? No. But the truth, so help me.

I Promise to Love, Honor, and Encourage You No Matter How Weird Your Life Gets

I believe I've already mentioned this, but this entire writing gig is a complete surprise to both Eric and me. *We did not see this coming.* When we first married, we envisioned a life that was more, I don't know, balanced, maybe? I thought I'd have a normal job, and he'd have a normal job, and together we'd raise a couple of kids and split all the household chores. This is exactly what we did for a long time, until I quit my job a few years ago to write and volunteer.

I don't know what you'd call what we're doing now, but *balanced* doesn't come close. If you put me in a dress and an apron, I honestly don't know if you could tell the difference between me and June Cleaver. Have I gone to work recently? No. Have I ironed a tablecloth recently? Yes.*

Want more proof? How long do you think it's been since Eric did a load of laundry? It's been about a year. But let me tell you what, Eric doesn't have much time to do laundry because he's working a million hours a week. (Don't tell his mother. She worries.)

Finances and 1960s social politics aside, I could not write and blog if it wasn't for Eric's encouragement and support. At least once a week I storm out of our room and harrumph—"I quit! I'm getting a job!" Sometimes I do this because the budget is tight or I want something expensive. Sometimes we have two broken-down cars and aren't sure how we will afford a new one when we need one. Sometimes I just get fed up with the blogging or the sales or whatever, and I just want to quit.

But Eric never lets me. He always drags me right back to the point, which is that I *can't* quit. I have a calling that is higher than busted cars or fancy dining room sets or even paying for braces. Perhaps you have the exact same sort of calling Eric has—you need to be the one who supports and encourages someone else who has a challenging calling. You might get to live a relatively steady and sane life because God knows you need some extra mental energy to keep your loved one from going off the deep end.

This isn't just true in marriages. Adoptive parents need prayer and people to buy the things they sell to raise money. Missionaries need someone to stay at home and make some serious money so they can have the financial support they need to do the job

---

* I only ironed the tablecloth because it was Christmas Day and we were having a very nice dinner with family. Don't think I make a habit of this.

they've been called to do. Someone needs to be the goer, and someone needs to be the giver. Your calling might be the supporting role, so embrace your position and give for all you're worth.

In Luke 8:1–3 there's a tiny little mention of this very idea. Jesus was traveling around with a small troop of followers. The twelve apostles were there, of course, but also a few women: Mary, Joanna, Susanna, and a few others who aren't specifically named. Verse 3 says: "These women were helping to support them out of their own means." These women supported *Jesus* in his ministry. Their supportive roles were crucial to our Lord! This is still true today; support and encouragement are crucial to successful ministries.

A Group-Wide Calling

What's better than a good friend? How about a whole group of good friends? The body of Christ is called to support one another in all things so the name of God may be honored. When we unite and strengthen each other, the body is a stronger unit. When our body is a stronger, healthier unit, the world notices. When the world notices, God's name is honored. It's not just about us but also about God receiving the glory.

When we take the time to develop healthy, Christian friendships, then we are living life as the early church did. In Acts 2:44–46 Luke says, "All the believers were together and had everything in common. They sold their property and possessions to give to anyone who had need. Every day they continued to meet together in the temple courts. They broke bread in their homes and ate together with glad and sincere hearts." These people needed one another because they were living in uncharted territory. They were about to suffer persecution and blessing unlike anything they had ever seen before. Think of what their lives would have been like if they had lived them alone! As a group, they could encourage one another and grow stronger in the Lord. Alone, they might not have made it! Satan does so love to find us alone and vulnerable. Don't give the devil that chance—develop those strong Christian friendships!

Do you have a group of friends who encourage one another? I certainly do hope so. Ideally church is the first place to connect to other believers. There are small groups, work groups, classes, and fun trips. All this togetherness in the name of Christ brings us closer. When hard times hit, and they will, you have a built-in support group.

The group doesn't need to be from your church, of course. Our friends from college are still some of our closest friends. They encourage us toward God's goals for our lives, even when our only contact is every four years at a wedding or checking in on Facebook. Perhaps you have neighbors who are Christians or friends at school. It doesn't matter where they are, as long as there is a united group that has a common purpose to encourage one another toward the goals God gives us.

Abandon Ship! Abandon Ship! No, Wait. Bail Out the Ship!

I'm not saying that you have to abandon all your non-Christian friends. Quite the contrary—you may be the only person who can show them Christ! Your calling may be to bring as many of your friends as possible to God. There is, however, a balance. If you don't have enough Christian friends encouraging and teaching you, you may find yourself in the precarious position of being influenced by the world instead of you being the one doing the influencing. Take the first steps of going and finding good Christian friends. Pray that God will lead you to people who can be healthy, supportive sisters and brothers in Christ while you reach out together to non-Christians.

Our pastor, Jason, does this really well. He loves hanging out with the unchurched, building genuine friendships. One of his passions is disc golf, and on the weekends you can find Jason out with a group of hoodlums,* roaming through the woods on a disc golf course. These men are not refined. They do not wear church pants or parrot church phrases. Jason reports a lot of swearing, some bawdy stories, and a wee bit of imbibing the fruit of the vine. Well, the fruit of the barley, more like. I don't think anyone is wandering through the woods with a good bottle of red.

Eventually the conversation will come around to what he does for a living, and he smiles and announces that he's a minister. At this point everyone stops what he's been doing for an hour and shifts from foot to foot. And Jason just keeps going, being the perfectly normal person he's been for the afternoon. They get to know him as a man who cares about them, who can play a decent game of disc golf, and who also happens to have a deep and living faith.

Romans 10:14–15 says: "How, then, can they call on the one they have not believed in? And how can they believe in the one of whom they have not heard? And how can they hear without someone preaching to them? And how can they preach unless they are sent? As it is written, 'How beautiful are the feet of those who bring good news!'" So our question today is this—how beautiful are our feet? Are they bringing anyone good news? Or are we only hanging out with people who already have the good news?

I have one final thought on this matter. We talked about Ruth and Naomi sticking together and eventually being part of a crucial portion of history. If we combine that idea with the idea of reaching out to the lost, do you know what explosive kind of life

---

* *Hoodlums* might be a strong word. I think they're just normal guys. But I love the word *hoodlum* and wanted to work it into the book at least once. I feel better now.

change you could witness? What if that guy you play disc golf with on Saturdays becomes a Christian after you invite him to church, and then he goes on to become the next Billy Graham? What if millions of lives are changed because you get to know that guy with the disc and the beer can in the woods?

You never can tell what God has planned.

Obviously, I Am a Better Christian Than You Are

I'd like to skip this section because I'm a big fan of denial. I like to live in my imaginary world of rainbows and unicorns and fuzzy sweaters by the fire. But if we're going to talk about supportive and encouraging friendships, we also need to talk about the dark side—the destructive and disheartening relationships. Sometimes Christians are as friendly as a pack of crotchety wolves. We can quietly try to one-up each other in the holiness department. Sometimes we aren't even quiet about it, and that's usually when we find ourselves in a screaming church split, encouraging the community to point and whisper about what a mess we are.

Somehow we lose sight of the purpose of encouragement and how each of us has a different call from God. He doesn't have the exact same plan for everyone! If we are truly encouraging a friend, we will look at him or her with love, not criticism. We might ask questions if we don't understand what our friends are doing or why, but the love we have for them should override our opinion of what they're doing. We must focus on building one another up so God can be glorified in all we do. Romans 15:1–6 gives us this example to follow, where we find no excuses for selfishness or condemnation:

> We who are strong ought to bear with the failings of the weak and not to please ourselves. Each of us should please our neighbors for their good, to build

them up. For even Christ did not please himself but, as it is written: "The insults of those who insult you have fallen on me." For everything that was written in the past was written to teach us, so that through endurance taught in the Scriptures and the encouragement they provide we might have hope. May the God who gives endurance and encouragement give you the same attitude of mind toward each other that Christ Jesus had, so that with one mind and one voice you may glorify the God and Father of our Lord Jesus Christ.

Let's be honest here. Can we ever really know what God is saying to one of His other children? Obviously, there are specific biblical principles we all need to obey. There are sins that will always be sins, and there are good choices that will always be blessings. But short of those specific directives, there are a lot of things that are just between a child and the Father. So what might look like failure or slacking from the outside might be *none of our business.*

Our business is to encourage one another. Love one another. Pray for one another! Snarkiness, judgmental attitudes, and criticism are simply not options. (Just for the record, those last things do fall clearly into the sin category.)

If you find yourself surrounded by disheartening relationships, there's only so much you can do. Maybe you've tried being the positive, loving member, but nothing changed. There might come a point when the negative attitudes of others become poisonous and you need to remove yourself from the situation.

If you've given it a good try and have still formed no friendships, then try another church. Try another ministry. I'm not encouraging church-hopping, especially for your own social pleasure, but sometimes friendships just aren't working out or aren't growing deep. Don't be too quick to run out on the family of God and the relationships that need to develop within the family, but there's no sense in sitting around sucking in poison either.

Jesus Didn't Do It Alone Either

Our lives are meant to be lived in cohesion with others. We support each other, we encourage each other, and we lend each other money when it's time for lunch but one of us is broke. The best way to do that and accomplish God's will is to make sure that our supporters and encouragers are also Christians with the same goal. God's name will be blessed when we work together.

Even Jesus, the perfect Son of God, knew this. Right after John baptized Him and He started to preach, He began to gather His disciples. Could He have done it on His own, with only the Father's companionship? Of course! But He didn't want to. He wanted encouraging friends by His side to share the journey. I think that's still a great plan two thousand years later.

STUDY QUESTIONS

1. Do you have any great friends you met after a huge life change? Who are they, and how have they had an impact on your life? How have you affected their lives?

2. Do you hesitate to obey God because you fear leaving friends and family? How do you think God will work through this problem if you choose to obey Him?

3. Think of your closest group of friends. How can you encourage one another to obey and serve God?

4. How can you develop more Christian friendships?

5. Do you have any non-Christian friends you can influence for Christ? Name an issue that you can specifically pray about for them this week. Also, name a way you can reach out to them in a tangible way.

6. Look up the following Scripture verses and consider how godly friendships helped to bring about God's glory:

    a. 1 Samuel 20:1–17
    b. Daniel 3:13–30
    c. Acts 16:16–34

Cheri Swalwell Balances a Home-Based Business and Writing

Cheri Swalwell works from home so she can earn the income her family needs—while still being available for them. As if a home business, a husband, and three children aren't enough, a few years ago she felt God asking her to write for Him. She started off intermittently, writing as she had time. Each new step of the writing process has been a learning opportunity and a new chance to be flexible. Each new step has also required that she listen carefully for her new instructions. This is what she said about her adventure:

I came home from a writing conference with a plan. I told God I was ready to have a full-time writing career within two years. He probably laughed at my plan, but at the time I was completely serious. I thought two years was plenty of time to get things rolling and have a writing career, balanced perfectly with my family responsibilities. Things have not worked out with the timing I had envisioned.

Throughout this process God has changed things some. He gave me the opportunity to publish two nonfiction books in November 2012 and December 2012 respectively, and that was definitely a learning experience. The books are no longer with that publishing company, but I learned so much about the process. I needed that experience to gain self-confidence to head in the direction God has planned for us. As a result, I'm getting ready to self-publish my third book and hope to complete several more self-published books next year.

There have been many new learning experiences already, with more to come. I have to learn how to self-publish, I have to learn marketing, I have to learn how to video blog, and I want to learn about making apps. There is a lot I have to learn about (including technology), but that's okay. God will provide the avenues to learn, and God will provide the means if that is the direction He wants me to take.

I'm much more flexible now than I was before. I used to say, "I don't want to work outside the home. I don't want to do X, but I'm willing to do Y and Z." Now I realize that whatever God is asking of me, even if it may be hard, will be better in the long run than not doing what He wants me to do. It's exciting to walk the path *with* God as my friend and Father instead of spouting off "my will" and "my desires" and asking Him to be the genie with the magic lamp. I'm a much better follower than leader anyway.

Throughout this entire process, God has been front and center. I feel He is leading me away from fiction toward nonfiction and speaking. I truly have a desire to encourage and inspire women (and men, but mainly women)—seekers, nonbelievers, and believers. I may go back to fiction someday, but I will need to work hard at the craft because coming up with a story is just the beginning. Being able to tell the story in a way that captures the attention of a reader is definitely something to be learned.

When I asked Him if I really heard Him right about a speaking/writing career, I said, "Lord, I need a message if I'm going to speak for you." He gave me one message within a few weeks of that prayer, and He has since given me another message. I don't have all the details filled in, but the basic messages are there. That's exciting to me because I feel these are messages people desperately need to hear. Each one brings God glory, not me.

I also don't feel that now is the time for me to begin a speaking ministry. I'm still in the preparation phase, and that's okay. I resisted the "preparation phase" for a while, but I'm grateful for it now. I know that when God finally says, "It's time to move," I need to be ready, and by His grace, He's giving me that time now.

God doesn't call us to an easy life, but the life He calls us to is peaceful when we're doing what He wants of us. I've made plenty of mistakes, but those mistakes helped me in the long run. I'm grateful that God loves me enough to keep working on changing me into who He wants me to be. That's an exciting place to me.

And as I love to say, "What He's willing to do for me, He's waiting to do for you too, if you just ask." I'm not special—just loved. ■

CHAPTER 11

Welcoming Weakness

2 CORINTHIANS 12:9-10

But he said to me, "My grace is sufficient for you, for my power is made perfect in weakness." Therefore I will boast all the more gladly about my weaknesses, so that Christ's power may rest on me. That is why, for Christ's sake, I delight in weaknesses, in insults, in hardships, in persecutions, in difficulties. For when I am weak, then I am strong."

Let's get it all out in the open. Let's list every excuse we can think of for not accomplishing what God is asking us to do:

- Physical/Mental Infirmities: depression, back pain, gout, mental illness, stomach trouble, food allergies, blindness, hairiness, obesity
- Life Stuff: pregnancy, small children, no children, divorce, disdain of people in general, lack of intelligence, lack of social skills, lack of money, bad family history, old age, youthfulness
- Career Stuff: busyness, previous commitments, need for more income, lack of the right college degree, retirement too far away . . .

There. I've exhausted my brain, and I'm sure I haven't even thought of a tenth of the excuses God hears every day. Some of these He hears from my own lips! I have celiac disease, and I can't eat any wheat. I can't have wheat touch my food. I have to wash my hands after I make my kids a sandwich. This is handy whenever I think of going on a mission trip. I'd either have to survive on hardboiled eggs and apples for a week, or I'd have to lump it and survive with round after round of Pepto-Bismol until my digestive system finally gave up and killed me. This is what I tell myself, anyway. I might be fine if I went to a country where they don't eat much wheat. But until I learn how to say, "Dear waiter, has any wheat been in contact with this food?" in Mandarin, I'm sticking with my story.

I tried and tried to think of a Bible story that supports my theory about excuses, and I can't think of one. I can think of *all* of them. The whole Bible is full of story after story of ordinary people God used for extraordinary things: liars, murderers, adulterers, scaredy cats, sick people, old people, nerds, hookers, pig-sloppers, divas, and lepers. The weakness did not matter. The illness did not matter. The fear did not matter.

In fact, that was God's entire point. Without Him, they could do nothing. It still is God's point! We are small and insignificant, but God is going to be there, directing our paths, strengthening us, and moving us forward.

That last paragraph was meant to be inspirational. Sort of a "Get up and get moving with God" call to action. I realize that it may have the opposite effect on you, and now you're even more afraid of what God might be asking of you and how weak you really might be. You're frozen to your couch, too feeble to move. Don't worry, my friend. By the end of this chapter you'll be off the couch, running for your keys so you can get moving with God. His strength is amazing like that.

God's Greatness Is Shown by Our Smallness

God is very smart. He knows that anytime we accomplish something on our own we automatically take the credit and get a big head. This is a sad but true fact for nearly everyone in the human race. "Look at what I did!" we shout. Genuine and pure pride in doing something well is a great feeling, and it's okay to be pleased with something we've done. However, God wants us to look at Him. To give *Him* the credit. To acknowledge *His* provision, strength, and love. I believe this is why He allows us to experience a myriad of weaknesses and problems that seem to make His calling impossible.

Let's think back to our friend Moses. Do you remember all those excuses he rolled out before God? He couldn't speak well, he wasn't a leader, no one was going to listen to him. Was he wrong? No! No one would have listened to Moses if God hadn't been working through him.

God first spoke to Moses in Exodus 3. God started speaking, and Moses promptly started making excuses. Moses was well aware of his weaknesses; he was well aware of the reality he faced. As the story continued, his fears proved true. He tried to convince the Israelites and Pharaoh that God was speaking, but *no one* would listen to him. His own people were upset with him because the Egyptians were making their lives even harder. And Pharaoh wasn't convinced by Moses' miracles. Everything he had feared was coming true right in front of his eyes. No ability to lead. No ability to convince. Nothing!

Moses had a GIANT call from God, and He had God's full assurance that something amazing was about to happen, but *nothing was happening*. He was getting guff from everyone. Exodus 6:9 says, "Moses reported this [God's promise] to the Israelites, but they did not listen to him because of their discouragement and harsh labor." He was floundering, and I'm sure his weaknesses were screaming in his face. "Give up, go home; raise some sheep. You're good at sheep, Moses. This isn't working out so well."

I don't know why God let Moses feel so powerless and weak. But I do realize that when He decided the time was right for some serious miracles, Moses must have rejoiced. Can you imagine the electricity that shot through Moses every time God spoke to him and allowed him to work a miracle? When they were convincing Pharaoh with that little miracle routine using the snakes and the blood and the frogs, I think Moses was surprised over and over again.

He knew he was unable to change anyone's mind. But God could change everyone's mind with just a few waves of His almighty hand. Even Moses changed his mind! Partway through the story Moses stopped making excuses and started working with God like it was natural. He finally found his strength in God's strength, and God's people walked out of Egypt into His freedom.

I notice this one thing—Moses never gave up. He might have been afraid, frustrated, and baffled, and common sense would have ordered him home to the sheep. But he kept going! He stayed right with God, talking to God, working with God. And God's strength did not fail. He won't fail in our situation either.

If We're Paralyzed by the Big Things, Let's Work on the Little Things Instead

I know the problems can seem paralyzing. I know you may be thinking that God's strength in our weakness is a fine theory, but it really doesn't fit your circumstances. I will not pretend to have inside knowledge on your particular situation. For all I know, you're facing down a doozy of a set of problems. But I am confident that the Bible is true for all who read it and believe, and there is no contradicting the fact that God calls us to continually grow in Him, in biblical understanding, and in love for our fellow humans. Even when the big things seem to be out of our control, possibly even out of God's control,* we can refocus our efforts on the manageable things.

* Just for the record, things are never out of God's control. But it certainly does seem like it sometimes from our perspective, doesn't it?

Each of us is capable of understanding the Bible and doing our best to love God and others. We can be encouraging, we can pray and read the Bible, and we can be kind to our families. All these things are good. In fact, if you are overwhelmed at the idea of God having a plan for your life or if your weaknesses are ruling the day, this may be the first place to start. God may just want you to start with the basics. There's no point in running to the missions field if you can't be kind to your sister. You might need to start small and work toward the big stuff. Do you remember that in the first chapter we talked about how Jesus commanded us to love God and to love others, and He also gave us the Great Commission to make disciples of all people? What might seem to be the smallest steps—speaking kindly when we're irritated, choosing to be humble when we'd like to be anything but—these are actually the big things.

Have you ever tried to spend the day with a person who tries your patience? I mean, really, you can't imagine surviving consecutive hours with this person, but for some reason you have to do it anyway. Don't you need every bit of the Holy Spirit's grace to get through the day? Maybe it's just me, but that one little command to love others undoes me *every time*. My weakness is profound even in this simple command; even the minimal things show God's greatness in our lives.

When I come up against these difficult (but relatively minor) problems, I have a few options. I can lean on my own strength and fail *miserably*. If I have to spend an entire day with a person who tries my patience, without God's help I will be the nastiest, crankiest woman on the planet by the end, because I am a big fan of pleasant, well-mannered people and personal time. Or, I can start praying fervently as soon as the challenge begins and watch God's grace smooth the day over. He soothes my spirit, He shows me how to love this person, and He sometimes even lets me take a nap in the middle of the day to coast through a few of the lagging hours. (Right now all my friends are trying to remember if I napped when we were together last time.)

If we start with the manageable areas, we're taking those baby steps we need to achieve an active life of faith. Those baby steps might be the only things we bring to this entire process. Honestly, there are going to be some parts of this calling that are well beyond your control. It looks like adopting two children from India is impossible because *it is impossible*. For us, anyway. We can't conjure up the money or the visas or the diplomatic approval any more than we can conjure up a loaf of bread on the moon. This is beyond us. Our weakness points to God's strength, and we get to be part of the experience. And when we finally have those babies home in our arms, guess who gets all the glory? Not us, that's for sure.

Our Weaknesses Are Often Our Ministries

This point is going to be about as much fun as a fork in the eye, but I'd be remiss not to bring it up. There are times when our assignment from God is directly related to our greatest weakness. I know you may not want to stand on a mountaintop and shout out that your body is weak, that your brain is unwell, or that you've made horrible choices in the past. Take time to pray about it and make sure God is really asking you to use this portion of your life. You may have a special story to share with others who desperately need to hear it. I have heard messages from women who have had abortions, adults who were raised in abusive homes, and drug addicts who have recovered. There is nothing as powerful as a person who can, through God's power, take a problem and turn it around for good.

Don't be afraid to start small. Perhaps you just need to share with one person confidentially. Then another, then another. God will bring you the people He needs you to touch as long as your heart is in the right place. If you're still terrified, maybe you'd feel better if you researched other people who are sharing a story similar to yours. What are they saying? Who is being helped? What kind of a reaction have they had? You aren't the only one with a difficult story to tell, and don't let Satan convince you that you are. Other people may need to hear you, and your story may give them the courage to seek Christ's healing.

In the chapter on sin, we talked about this concept—about how we might be able to use our past as a connection point for others. We can extend this idea to things other than sin—any weakness or struggle, really. Mental illness, tough family life, terrible financial circumstances, physical illness—anything can be used to reach others for God.

Do you remember the story of Rahab the harlot? Her story in Joshua 2 isn't exactly one of purity and light. First of all, she was a prostitute. My NIV study note mentions that Josephus and other early writers refer to her as an "innkeeper," not a harlot. But I took out my NIV concordance and looked up the word, and I am fairly confident that we are looking at a woman who was sexually welcoming, not just hospitable. Well past your average services for an innkeeper, we'll say. We don't know what motivated this woman to offer these services, but one can assume that most women do not fall into this career because it sounds fun. There was probably a long and complicated list of reasons why she did what she did. Her weaknesses and challenges helped to define who she became for a time, but not forever.

Not only was Rahab a prostitute with a complicated story, but she was also sort of a liar. The two spies stayed at her house while they checked out the land. The king of Jericho wasn't excited about the spying, so he sent some messengers to her house to retrieve the Israelites. Here is what Rahab told them (Joshua 2:4–6):

"Yes, the men came to me, but I did not know where they had come from." (Probable lie. But I can't prove it. Maybe she didn't know right away.)

"At dusk, when it was time to close the city gate, they left." (Huge lie. But an effective one, because she included some details to make it plausible.)

"I don't know which way they went." (Liar, liar, pants on fire. She knew exactly where they were because she put them on the roof.)

"Go after them quickly. You may catch up with them." (Now we've moved from lying to manipulative suggestions. Nice.)

We can get into a long discussion about gray areas here, because even though we are supposed to tell the truth, there are times when a little subterfuge like Rahab's may just save someone's bacon. Her caginess worked, the men moved out looking for the spies where the spies couldn't possibly have been, and she moved to Part 2 of her plan—saving her own bacon.

She may have been a harlot, but she was a smart harlot. Rahab and the spies agreed on a signal to ensure her family's safety when the rest of Israel returned to take down Jericho. But in the middle of her plotting she offered this surprisingly heartfelt plea to the men:

> "I know that the LORD has given you this land and that a great fear of you has fallen on us, so that all who live in this country are melting in fear because of you. We have heard how the LORD dried up the water of the Red Sea for you when you came out of Egypt, and what you did to Sihon and Og, the two kings of the Amorites east of the Jordan, whom you completely destroyed. When we heard of it, our hearts melted and everyone's courage failed because of you, for the LORD

your God is God in heaven above and on the earth
below. Now then, please swear to me by the LORD that
you will show kindness to my family, because I have
shown kindness to you." (Joshua 2:9–12)

I think that's where Rahab's story made a radical turn for the
good. She understood where her focus needed to be, and it was
right on the power of God. She believed the Lord could dry up
a sea and command the heavens above and the earth below, and
she was certain that the Lord could also work on her behalf. She
sought kindness from the men who professed to believe in the
Almighty, and it was not denied her. Rahab's family was spared
in the fall of Jericho, and she also went on to be a hero of the
faith. She's listed in Hebrews 11 with the other men and women
who believed God no matter how impossible the dream may
have been.

Now, this example isn't perfect, because we don't know that
Rahab started an outreach to former prostitutes, or even to former truth-benders. But we do know that she must have turned
a powerful corner and looked beyond her past, beyond her own
weaknesses. She could have focused only on her bad choices and
personal problems, and she could have died in the fall of Jericho with everyone else. Instead, God honored her faith in His
strength and used her in a powerful way. Will we allow Him to
do the same with us?

Pride Is Never Useful

Feeling weak and wimpy isn't fun, but it's better than suffering
from delusions of grandeur. At least weakness keeps us humble.
Imagine with me the following scenario from New Testament
times: Let's say that Jesus ignored the fishermen and normal
people and went directly to the temple to find His disciples. He

could have chosen the most educated men in the country. He could have picked men who knew the Old Testament forward and backward and had the important robes to show it.

Can you imagine what a disaster that would have been? He would have spent three years fighting their pride, their knowledge, and their self-righteous attitudes. They were exactly the opposite of what He needed, which was twelve normal men who would trust and obey even when they were clueless. Ta-da! If that sounds like you, then we're in business.

I cannot tell you how many days I have considered giving up writing for something "normal." I don't know what I'm doing here! I don't have a theological background, which becomes evident every time my pastor and I start talking about the Bible. Great is Jason's reward in heaven for the long emails he types out to me (on his iPhone, no less) just so what I write is biblically consistent. I don't have a background in writing or literature or any of those subjects that would be helpful for actually writing books. I don't have a technical background, so when I go to learn about blogging and SEOs and Twitter, my eyes roll back in my head. I wander into the kitchen for chocolate to calm my frustration.

Yet God doesn't care about any of this. My weakness just gives Him more opportunity to show His strength. God loves the humble, clueless, lost, trusting, and obedient types. They're often the only ones who get anything done the way He wants. Not that we aren't smart and capable, but we know that He is so much smarter and more capable than we are! And hallelujah for that. Psalm 150:1–2 echo my thoughts: "Praise the LORD. Praise God in his sanctuary; praise him in his mighty heavens. Praise him for his acts of power; praise him for his surpassing greatness."

Amen!

The Glory Must Always Be His

If we do anything in the name of Christ and the glory comes back to rest on ourselves, then it is all for naught. No matter what we do, we must make sure that we give credit to God whenever possible. If people ask, we must tell them about God's provision. If we speak, we speak in His name. If we act out in love, then we act because of Christ. Our weaknesses and challenges give us prime opportunities to let His strength work through us, ensuring He gets all the glory He deserves.

When we give God the glory and a chance to work through us, our weaknesses somehow disappear. I'm not sure how this happens, but I have yet to see it fail. Remember, God loves us even when we are weak, but He is never impressed with prideful hearts.

STUDY QUESTIONS

1. List all your weaknesses that may inhibit you from doing something God would ask of you.

2. Which of these weaknesses are actual problems, and which are just excuses?

3. Imagine what God can do if you hand over the weakness to Him and let Him work through it. Think about this prayerfully several times this week.

4. Do you have a strength that may actually inhibit God's ability to work through you? What is it? What can you do to turn that strength over to God's work?

5. Look up the following verses and write them down. Post them someplace you can see them:
   a. 2 Corinthians 4:7
   b. 2 Corinthians 12:9–10
   c. 2 Peter 1:3

David's weaponry was ridiculous: a sling and five stones. It didn't matter. God still uses foolish tools in the hands of weak people to build His kingdom. Backed by prayer and His power, we can accomplish the unthinkable.

Jim Cymbala, *Fresh Wind, Fresh Fire*

Simon Preaches Even When He Thinks He Has Nothing to Offer

Here Simon tells a story about how obeying God can be just plain messy. Even when it's hard, even when we don't understand, even when we feel like we have nothing to offer, we still need to listen.

I guess it was about two years ago now. It was one of those days that had escalated from moment one. My wife suffers terribly from fibromyalgia. She has good days and bad, but every once in a while she has a really bad day that affects everyone else.

On one particular day everything went haywire. Laura was at the end of her rope. The girls had made her angry, we had argued, bills had not been paid. We had a big, big mess at home.

It was then, right in the middle of my wife just losing it, with me and my daughters standing around, that my wife said, "Well, I might as well just take the WHOLE BOTTLE!" She literally attempted to swallow a whole bottle of hydrocodone! As soon as she got the pills in her mouth, both of my girls screamed *"No, Momma!"* and Kristen jumped her, knocked her to the ground, and both started scooping wet pills from her mouth.

Where was I? In utter shock and amazement! It happened so quickly, I never reacted. Praise God for two young girls!

Now, what's the point of this? Well, first of all, I am a pastor. Pastors never have problems, do they? At least none we can share with anyone. I felt absolutely, 100 percent alone at that moment. There was literally no one I could call or talk to. My fears overwhelmed me, and I worried about what would happen to our family if anyone found out. It was one of the darkest times of my life, and hardly anyone knows about it. The worst part—*the worst part*—was that this was less than an hour before I had to preach on a Wednesday night.

What did I do? Well, first of all, I wept. Then I prayed. Then I thought, "How am I supposed to stand behind a pulpit at a time like this? But then again, what am I supposed to do!?" I felt I HAD to preach! It was too late for excuses or finding a replacement, and I had no reason for one either (at least one I could tell).

I had to do what God had called me to do. I had to obey.

As I walked to church, across the parking lot from our house, all I could think about was that I had no sermon, no message, and practically no guarantee anything would be okay. All I knew was that I was where God wanted me, that people were expecting to hear me preach, and that I had to say something. I hoped it was what God wanted me to say.

I went on in, church started, and finally I got up to preach. That's when it hit me . . . this could be a battle of spiritual warfare. I had no intention of letting the devil win. I figured, based on past experiences, that there must have been a reason for what had just happened—why God allowed our family to go through what we did. So, I preached. I preached on the value of life, the gift of life, how precious life is—if for no other reason than God loved us so much that He would give Jesus as a ransom for our souls. Our value is based on the price that was paid for us—so that makes us priceless. Therefore, I said, suicide is the most wasteful act anyone could ever commit. Jesus loves us and died for us.

So, to wrap this up, my wife does not even remember why she did it, not at all. But at the end of that service, three different people came up to me—all three had been contemplating suicide! All thanked me for the message; they said it must have been God.

Yep. ■

CHAPTER 12

Breaking Nana's Heart

MATTHEW 10:37-39

Anyone who loves their father or mother more than me is not worthy of me; anyone who loves their son or daughter more than me is not worthy of me. Whoever does not take their cross and follow me is not worthy of me. Whoever finds their life will lose it, and whoever loses their life for my sake will find it.

Is there anything worse than knowing you've disappointed someone? I hate that. I hate letting a person down, no matter how little I know him or her. Last year I accidentally missed a due date and didn't pay the Internet bill on time. Certainly I *meant* to pay it, but I think the envelope was accidentally thrown away in a stack of paperwork, or something. It doesn't matter what happened; all that matters is that my stomach fell a foot when I realized my mistake. Wasting no time, I went online (fortunately they hadn't cut us off yet), paid it with our debit card, and set up automatic payments for future bills. Then I called the company to make contact with a real person, letting her know I had paid it and that it wouldn't happen again. You should have heard the dear woman on the other end of the line. She was professional about it, but it was clear that she wanted to recommend increasing my daily dose of Xanax or other anti-anxiety medicine of choice. I guess not everyone calls hyperventilating when they're a week overdue on their Internet bill.

As much as we want to please the people around us, we might have to reconsider that desire when God gives us instructions. Priorities. It all comes down to priorities. When we are old and decrepit in our beds, waiting to pass on, what are we going to look back and remember? Are we going to remember that we stepped out boldly and worked for that new ministry? That we spent generous amounts of time with the kids when they were small? That we gave up the well-paying job to work in the nonprofit? When I'm on my deathbed, I want to look back and remember that I was obedient and that I lived a life that *mattered*. And I wanted it to matter by God's standards, not human standards.

I don't want to look back and think, "Well, I made Mom happy, at least."* As important as relatives and friends are, there are many people who don't automatically encourage us to follow God's abundant plan. They first think of security and safety; second, of success; and third, of happiness. "God's Plan" ranks somewhere around "Save the Earth" or "I Want World Peace." It's a nice thought but not really practical. "God's Plan" doesn't sound like something that's going to put food on the table or a Cadillac in the garage or send the grandkids to a good school.

They are right, of course. God's plan often involves small houses, old cars, giving away money, and eating beans and rice three times a week. It can be tough when you disappoint people who love you but who just don't get it. Even if they've attended church for eighty-five years, they still might not get it. Don't let disappointment from others stop you, because your eternal reward is not going to come from Grandma.

)))   **Don't let disappointment from others stop you, because your eternal reward is not going to come from Grandma.**

The apostle Paul probably understood this even though he didn't say anything in the Bible about his family. Wouldn't it be

---

* For the record, my mother is a lovely woman who supports my efforts to follow God. She never harasses me about this writing thing, ever. Not once.

great if Paul had written a letter to his grandmother? Galatians, Ephesians, Nana, Philippians . . . Ha! I love it! It could have gone like this:

Paul, an apostle, your third grandson by your son Samuel,

To Nana and Uncle Eli:

Grace and peace to you from God our Father and the Lord Jesus Christ, whom you still disregard, but whom I believe to be the Savior of humankind.

I love you, but please stop sending me news clippings of the Pharisees. I know you were so proud that I had achieved status in the community, but I had to leave that life behind entirely. I know you aren't excited that I've become a wandering preacher. I know you're furious that I've been jailed repeatedly. I know Aunt Esther is needling you at family dinners because everyone is gossiping about me.

I am genuinely pained that my life is causing you grief. However, I cannot ever go back to what I was. I've seen something higher; I've heard directly from God. I must continue with Him.

On a lighter note, my feet have been cold in this prison. If you could whip me up some new socks, I'd surely appreciate it. You can send them down with my brother Gideon when he brings the spring wool to the market.

The grace of my Lord, Jesus Christ, be upon you. I pray for you daily.

Love, Paul (and please stop crossing off my "P's" and changing them to "S's." I'm Paul now, not Saul.)

In Acts 22:3–11, Paul actually does recount the story of his conversion. (I mean, I didn't make this part up.) He says this:

I am a Jew, born in Tarsus of Cilicia, but brought up in this city. I studied under Gamaliel and was thoroughly trained in the law of our ancestors. I was just as zealous for God as any of you are today. I persecuted the followers of this Way to their death, arresting both men and women and throwing them into prison, as the high priest and all the Council can themselves testify. I even obtained letters from them to their associates in Damascus, and went there to bring these people as prisoners to Jerusalem to be punished. About noon as I came near Damascus, suddenly a bright light from heaven flashed around me. I fell to the ground and heard a voice say to me, "Saul! Saul! Why do you persecute me?"

"Who are you, Lord?" I asked.

"I am Jesus of Nazareth, whom you are persecuting," he replied. My companions saw the light, but they did not understand the voice of him who was speaking to me

"What shall I do, Lord?" I asked.

"Get up," the Lord said, "and go into Damascus. There you will be told all that you have been assigned to do." My companions led me by the hand into Damascus, because the brilliance of the light had blinded me.

Years later Paul was deeply sorry about all the things he had done—the persecution, the arrests, the killing. But at the time they occurred, he was quite sure he was doing the right thing, and his companions agreed. These men were a team, removing the social blight called the Way from their society. Paul's friends saw the light, but they didn't understand what Jesus was saying. They realized something big had happened, but even though they were *right there next to him*, they didn't get the same message. Everything changed in an instant, and they weren't prepared.

Literally out of the blue, Paul had suddenly received a new calling and a higher priority. His friends must have been confused. Possibly they were furious. "This is not the plan, man. What are you doing? We're supposed to be killing these people, not *becoming* these people!" I wonder if any of them ever believed and followed Christ as well.

We can't forget the people who had lovingly trained Saul all those earlier years to become the persecuting, arresting zealot he had become. *Someone* had made sure he had been well trained under Gamaliel. *Someone* had taught him that the Hebrew faith was the only way. And those *someones* were likely terribly disappointed when Saul saw the light and believed in Jesus. Saul saw the light, but they only saw a traitor. If not a traitor, than at least a nutcase. Who leaves this sort of tradition and social comfort for a reckless existence of prison, wandering, and occasional beatings?

As years passed, I wonder how their relationships with Paul changed. Did they eventually write him off as a lunatic? Were they able to see the truth of the Messiah? Paul gathered many friends and followers as he preached the message of the gospel, but he never addressed old family or friends in the letters we have. We don't know what became of his earlier relationships, but we do know that he moved full-steam ahead in service to Christ. Which is so like Paul—zealous to the core.

Obviously our own examples are going to be a bit more subtle. We will likely not be blinded when Jesus gives us a new life direction, stopping us from creating mayhem at lunch this afternoon. But it's important to recognize that we also have people in our lives who will be disappointed when we make decisions they don't agree with, or when we put ourselves in harm's way for a goal they don't understand, or when we refuse to cooperate with things they think are important. When we face their disappointment, what will we do? Will we stop everything God wants so we can make another human happy? Or will we ride out the discomfort of their disapproval and obey God?

If Paul's example isn't enough to convince you, let's run through a few others. Abraham left his home, then wandered around for a long time looking for the land God promised him. Noah built an ark no one thought was necessary. Elijah publically harassed the prophets of Baal to show God's power on Mount Carmel. Zacchaeus left a wealthy life of tax collecting to follow Jesus. All of these people followed God's call for their lives, and they all may have had loved ones in the background thinking they were nuts.

But they weren't nuts, and neither are you. Stay the course, because the blessings are going to be worth it.

Stepping Back to a Bigger Perspective

My friend Dewayne preached at church a few years ago, before his family left the United States to go to central Asia to be missionaries. In that sermon he managed to give a large-view perspective of the entire Bible in less than thirty minutes. Pretty impressive, no? One of his best points was that if you are wondering what God wants to do with your life, you may need to stop looking at *your* life. You may need to step back and look at what God is doing in the entire world and then see where you might fit into a much larger plan.

I know your family and friends may seem intimidating, but in the scope of the entire world, they aren't really all that scary. It all depends on where you place your focus. Dewayne also said that while he was in high school he was terrified to share the gospel with his fellow students. His church was very missions focused, and he knew the importance of sharing the gospel. He determined that if he couldn't share the gospel, he could at least pray for those who were brave enough to do what he was afraid to attempt. He started collecting mission updates and (as a teenage boy, mind you) would take them into his room and pray for the missionaries regularly.

Dewayne said that something happened that he was not expecting; as he focused on these brave missionaries, God changed his own heart. The Lord gave him a new perspective and a passion to share the gospel. Do you remember last chapter's discussion on weaknesses, where I encouraged you to start with the small and manageable things? This is exactly what I was talking about. Dewayne started small, focusing on something he could handle—praying for people. He got his heart in the right place, and then God worked miracles beyond what Dewayne could do for himself.

I encourage you to try Dewayne's tactic. Research and study the very thing that God is asking you to do. The more you learn about it, focus on it, and discover how God is working through it, the more attainable it will seem. It is likely that there are real, live people out there succeeding at similar things to what God has called you to do. Once you know what is possible with God, staring down your disapproving aunt and your three cousins in medical school at Thanksgiving dinner will be a piece of cake.

We all need a gentle reminder every once in a while that we aren't the center of the known universe. It might seem as if the world rises and falls based on our efforts, but really we're just a small piece of the worldwide plan. When we remember that and start with small steps of obedience, God can radically change our perspective and give us the courage to move past the disappointment of others.

This chapter started with Matthew 10:37–39, where Jesus was encouraging His followers to take up their cross to follow Him, no matter what sacrifice it meant for family and friends. "Whoever find their life will lose it, and whoever loses their life for my sake will find it," He said (Matthew 10:39). Just before that passage Jesus also said this:

"So do not be afraid of them, for there is nothing con-
cealed that will not be disclosed, or hidden that will
not be made known. What I tell you in the dark, speak
in the daylight; what is whispered in your ear, proclaim
from the roofs. Do not be afraid of those who kill the
body but cannot kill the soul. Rather, be afraid of the
One who can destroy both soul and body in hell. Are
not two sparrows sold for a penny? Yet not one of
them will fall to the ground outside your Father's care.
And even the very hairs of your head are all numbered. So don't be afraid; you are worth more than
many sparrows." (Matthew 10:26–31)

I don't love that part where Jesus tells His disciples not to
fear the people who can kill the body. I am actually *quite afraid of
people who can kill my body*, thank you very much. But when He
contrasted that piddly little fear against the true concern of the
One who can destroy both body and soul in hell, well, that puts
it all into perspective. Then He tempered His stern warning with
some gracious encouragement—all the hairs of our heads are
numbered, and God knows us intimately. He cares for us wildly!

Now *that* is proper focus. We're serving a God who has unlim-
ited power, and He loves us. How can we possibly worry about
disappointing anyone other than Him?

Loving the Family When You Possibly Want to Choke Them Instead

I know it can be tempting to discontinue all communication with
the family when things get difficult. (We will not discuss how I
know this.) Perhaps you've spent years trying to convince some
family members that they are blind to the truth. They have spent

years convincing you that you are going to starve or waste your life. Years of impasse are not pretty.

Before you shriek and hang up the phone in frustration, take a deep breath and remember that your perspectives are different. They really do want what's best for you, but they just don't have the same priorities. Remember Saul's friends—they were right there with him but didn't get the same message. Your friends and family may be just like Saul's. This does not give you an excuse to give up on them, and in fact, your obedience may be the only true contact they have with Christ. Continuing a healthy and respectful relationship may one day soften their hearts, and they may one day find Him. Don't give up! In the meantime, here are some practical applications:

▶ Do not assume that every conversation has to be laden with important messages from God. There is nothing more annoying than a person who is determined to sell you something you do not want. You will not wear your friends or family down. You will make them cranky, and they will avoid you. Let God's love show through you, and let them watch and wonder.

▶ Don't be afraid to ask about their job, their children, their house, their football team—whatever. These little conversations are all about building a lasting relationship. Let them know you care about them as people, not as just another gold star on your "Dragging Them to Jesus" chart hanging on the fridge door.

▶ Find a common ground. There has to be something you share, even if it's a love for the smell of Grandpa's pipe smoke. Don't let them start to believe that there is some huge, holy divide that is keeping you apart. Don't be afraid to be *real*, to be human.

▶ Keep your sense of humor. Yes, God's plan is important. But sometimes a gap can be bridged in an instant
when we remember to lighten up. Don't be afraid to
be a bit snarky or sarcastic, if the situation requires.
My family has bridged many a difficult dinner with
sarcasm and dry wit. We excel at it, frankly.

▶ Pray for them. Usually it's best to pray quietly, but
praying out loud at a family gathering can really get
some quick results. Please note—I don't mean embarrassing specifics. It's just nice to be included in a prayer,
and you might be surprised to find that your non-
Christian friends and family enjoy that you remember them when you talk to God. For example: Good
Thanksgiving blessing—"Thank you for Jon's new job,
Lord." Bad prayer—"Lord, please convict Jon of his
gambling habit." You get the picture.

▶ Have your answer ready when they are ready. There
may actually come a day when they are ready to hear
your side of the story, and all your crazy sacrifice may
make sense to them. It may not be for years, so you
have some time to think this through. Give God the
glory, and have a clear and simple explanation of the
gospel ready to share.

I Can't Hear You, Uncle Joe. God's Voice Is Just So Much Louder Than Yours

Most of us are fortunate to have loving friends and family who
really do want what's best for us. It's not that we don't appreciate their concern; it's that we need to have our focus on the
proper place so we can do what God calls us to do. They may take
issue with you for taking the kids out of public school to homeschool. They may fear you're not saving enough for retirement

on that puny salary as a preacher. They may be secretly furious that they paid for your college education and you're now "wasting" it by staying home with the kids. Refocus, refocus! Where is your reward coming from? Pleasing Grandma or pleasing the God who loves you?

Don't let their concern, frustration, or plans derail your obedience to God's call.

Love them, but love God more.

STUDY QUESTIONS

1. Name every person in your family who is going to be affected when you obey God's calling. Also, list how this is specifically going to affect them.

2. What can you do to make this transition easier for them? What will you have to leave up to God?

3. Where have you focused your perspective? Are you more afraid of your grandma, or of the consequences of not obeying God?

4. For those family members who think you're crazy: what small things can you do to build a happy and relaxed relationship?

5. Study the following passages. Consider how these words can help you build a healthy relationship with your family while you also obey God:

   a. Matthew 5:11–16

   b. Luke 6:37–42

WHEN THERE'S NO EASY WAY TO SAY IT:

Communication Born of Desperation (Results Not Guaranteed)

There's nothing worse than a book that's long on theory and short on practical steps. With that in mind, here are some ways to share surprising/disappointing/cataclysmic news with those you love. Use these only when you're really, truly desperate.

Telling your mother:
I find it best to sandwich this sort of news into other, more upsetting types of news from other people:

"Hey Mom, did you hear that Beth just got a tattoo? And also, I'm going to adopt three children from India. And did you hear that Chuck just got a speeding ticket on his motorcycle?"

Key steps: Speak loudly and clearly as you throw your siblings under the bus. Be quieter and mumble a little through your own issues.

Telling your father:
Keep it short and sweet. Make sure you are exiting the room/house/country as you speak:

"Dad, I'm moving to Iraq to be a missionary. See you at Easter!" (Cue sound of your revving engine and spinning tires on gravel driveway.)

Key steps: Don't give him time to argue. Do not answer phone for at least two days if he calls.

Telling your siblings:
Text them.
> "Selling house to become traveling preacher."
> *Key steps:* Throw phone into lake to avoid return texts.

Telling your elderly relatives:
Write one long and sweet letter to the most sympathetic elder. She will be on the phone in a hot minute, informing all the other members of her generation.
> "Dear Great-Aunt Ethel, blah blah blah, it turns out I am pregnant with our eighth baby, blah blah blah, I love you so much."
> *Key steps:* Avoid family reunion until this all blows over.

Telling your church family:
Use the official prayer request line to announce your news:
> "The Clemence family requests prayer as *the Lord* calls them to sell their house, buy an RV, and travel around the country while Jessie researches her next book."
> *Key steps:* Emphasize that God is calling you to this. Direct all concerned parties to take their arguments directly to Him. Let God explain himself if they hassle you.

Telling everyone else:
Throw it out there on Facebook:
> "Does anyone have a wok we can borrow? It turns out we're moving to Cambodia in June."
> *Key steps:* After you make your announcement, do not check your Facebook profile for fifty to sixty years. Make peace with communicating via other forms of social media. ▪

Anthony Goes to Romania (with a pack of gum)

Anthony shared this story about listening to God and watching God provide when there was no human way for it to happen.

Let me tell you about the time God led me to go on a mission trip in 1992, then miraculously gave me the exact amount of money I needed for the trip—just in time.

Sparing you all the minor details, let's just say that I needed money for tickets to Romania and back. First, the tickets unexplainably dropped to half price. But then the travel agent called me and told me he reserved the tickets, but he needed me to pay the money on Thursday. This was Tuesday, and I had no money. On Wednesday night our pastor asked for a special love offering to be taken up, never telling what it was needed for.

I needed $638 for my tickets . . . I got $638.10. My pastor said God threw in a pack of gum for the trip.

I got to see at least eighty people come to Christ when I preached in Romania that year. ◼

CHAPTER 13

Marching Bravely

MATTHEW 14:27–33

But Jesus immediately said to them: "Take courage! It is I. Don't be afraid."

"Lord, if it's you," Peter replied, "tell me to come to you on the water."

"Come," he said.

Then Peter got down out of the boat, walked on the water and came toward Jesus.

No fear. That's us. Just give us the instructions and we're out the door, God. Toodles.

We fear no beasts that may be waiting to maul and chew us. We fear no humans, not even Great-Aunt Greta, who wants to derail us with second-rate plans. We fear no sin, no devil, or weakness. We don't even fear *fear*.

And we are lying. We are scared to death. Worst of all, sometimes we don't even realize how afraid we are until, like Peter, we are in the middle of something amazing that God is doing. The adrenaline carries us along, we hop out of the boat, and we take a few squishy steps.

Then, *kaboom*, we look around and think, *"What am I doing out here? It's wet! There's no dirt under me! The only thing holding me up is Jesus, and He's not exactly holding my hand."* I'm not going to lie to you; this is not a good feeling. It's scary. However, it is rare when fright actually kills someone, so let's get a move-on. No time to waste! One-two! One-two!

)))   **It is rare when fright actually kills someone, so let's get a move-on.**

Turn with me to the book of Joshua, please. We're going to discuss Joshua and the walls of Jericho that came down because of the hard work of the Israelites. They took picks and axes and worked for months to destroy the walls. Whew! It was exhausting!

Or maybe not. The actual destruction of Jericho was ridiculous, the kind of ridiculous that's right up there with Noah having to build that ark. Why God didn't just blow Jericho out of the ground with a huge poof and some smoke, I do not know. He had another plan that included using a bunch of normal, scared people. However, what His plan lacked in common sense He more than made up for with drama, so we'll let Him have his way. (Ha ha, Lord! I made a funny!)

The rubble of Jericho is found in Joshua 6. But before we get to the wreckage, God had to spend a few chapters giving instructions and building up courage. Four times God told Joshua to be strong and courageous. God had to repeat it four times! It reminds me of when my son was little and could not wrap his mind around the concept of time. I would give him the itinerary for the day, and sometimes he had to wait all day for something super exciting, like going to McDonald's. I would say, "Remember, we aren't going out to eat until after Audrey gets home from school and Daddy gets home from work. Do you understand?" I'd say this over and over until he finally got it. Even then, things were dicey. Both of us were nervous wrecks by the time Daddy walked through the door.

God obviously thought that His little Hebrews were in need of repeated encouragement with their instructions before they stepped out in faith. In Joshua 1:5 God said this: "No one will be able to stand against you all the days of your life. As I was with

Moses, so I will be with you; I will never leave you nor forsake you." That relationship, that *connection*, is what should give us courage as we follow God. We are not doing this on our own!

Let's put this into an example. Let's say I decide to paint the outside of the house, and I want my little girl to do it with me. Would I hand her the paintbrush, then abandon her after the front door is done? "I'm done, now, honey. See that you're careful up there on the ladder. It's tricky around that chimney. And make sure you do it perfectly so the neighbors won't laugh at me."

I wouldn't do that to Audrey, and God certainly wouldn't do it to us! I'll be right next to my girl, showing her how to paint around the doorways, how not to slop the paint, and how not to kill my flowers while painting near them. As we reach each new step, I'll show her the way. She won't be left without directions when she needs them, but I won't tell her everything up front either. She wouldn't be ready for all the information. God does the same for us. He stays right with us, working through every step as it comes.

The Israelites must have been assured of God's presence after all his pep talks, so they stepped out in faith. That's pretty much all they did, unless you count the horn blowing and a little shouting on the last day. For six days in a row the people marched around the city of Jericho one time while the trumpets sounded. The seventh day they marched seven times, then they shouted while the trumpets blasted. The walls fell down. Simple as that, God used their obedience and courage to honor His own name, and a miracle occurred. It was obvious to all that His strength was to be credited, because the Israelites hadn't even touched the wall. Their courage resulted in obedience; their obedience opened the door for God to glorify himself.

Did they feel ridiculous? I'm guessing yes. Were they waiting for the flaming arrows to whiz through the air to kill them? Likely. Or maybe I'm completely wrong, and they were so full of faith they marched with confidence and joy. Joshua 6 simply relates that they were obedient with each step, never faltering from the instructions they'd been given. Obviously, I wasn't there, and I don't know for sure how they were feeling as they marched. But I do know that God did not let them down. Their courage was rewarded. A pile of rubble testified to the power behind a few courageous and obedient children.

The Point Where "Preparation" Becomes "Stalling"

Up to this point in the book we've been in planning and preparation mode. We've sorted out the financial aspects, we've had imaginary conversations in our heads with grumpy Great-Aunt Greta, and we've spent time praying and reading the Bible. We've learned all we can about God's plan for our lives, and we've confessed every sin we can think of. Maybe even some we didn't commit, but we want to make sure all the bases are covered.

These are all good things. Proper preparation is key.

However, remember the chapter on God's timing? Remember that we talked about how we can't run ahead of God, but we shouldn't lag behind Him either? Right about now the reality of your situation and calling may be starting to dawn on you. You've prepared as much as a human can prepare for anything, yet you still can't quite put things into motion. You're standing on the diving board, looking down at the water, but you can't bring yourself to jump.

Maybe that application sits on the desk in a pile of paperwork, or maybe you haven't had the guts to bring up the subject with your spouse, or maybe you just haven't hit the send button on the computer. There is one tiny little thing left to put this whole train into motion, but you just aren't quite brave enough to do it.

I get it. I really do. When I started writing, there wasn't much to be afraid of. I was completely sure the experiment was going to be an utter failure. So I mentioned to my husband that I was going to write a bit, he said that was nice, and I plopped down at the computer and did my thing. Expecting failure. Realists are very good at this.

To my surprise, the book I churned out wasn't so bad. (Heck, you're reading it right now.) So I did a little research, posted the book proposal to a website, and went about my normal life. I had been obedient, but there was nothing to lose. No one who knew me knew I had written the book, so none of it mattered. I might as well have knitted a scarf or perfected the art of pruning bonsai trees—I had a new hobby to entertain myself.

Telling friends and family that I had written a book tipped things into motion. At first I rarely said a word to anyone but my husband—not even to my own parents. Even to this day, I'm not sure why I began to tell anyone. I think I had to justify what I was doing with all my free time when Caleb was in preschool; someone must have asked. I certainly wouldn't have volunteered that information without prompting. (What's worse—having everyone think I'm a lazy bum or revealing that I was calling myself a writer?) That was where I jumped off the diving board. When I finally did tell a few people, I thought the worst was over. A few of them read the book online and told me it wasn't bad, and I continued on with my normal life.

One day an editor emailed me, asking me to submit the manuscript to her publishing house. Things got real very quickly.

Suddenly, I needed prayer and support—and in order to get that, I had to tell people. Here's the thing about prayer requests— *technically* you can ask for prayer without specifying the details. You can say something like, "I have a situation coming up this week, and I'd like everyone to pray about it. But I can't tell you what it is, exactly."

You can do this, but everyone in the room is going to spend the next three days obsessing about what dark secret you're hiding. Do you have a disease? Are your children rebelling? Are you going bankrupt? *Does your husband have a mistress named Tiffany who he's planning on running away with this week, leaving you with the mortgage, three kids, and a cat?*

Don't act like you don't know what I'm talking about.

So, to spare everyone the frustration of not knowing my deepest secrets, I had to come out and tell them.

Then I started a blog a year later, and I had to tell everyone about that. And then I started posting my blog posts to Facebook, and my life became an endless series of being brave enough to share what goes on in my head and what God speaks to my heart. An endless series of courageous choices.

I don't know why I felt like I was the only person on earth who needed to be courageous, because Matthew 14:22–33 tells a similar story. The disciples were out in a boat, and Jesus decided to meet them in the middle of the water. Well, why not? Why not break up the monotony of waiting for a boat to reach shore before climbing in? Obviously, the disciples had a nervous fit in the boat, what with the ghost walking toward them on the water. Jesus calmed them down, and this is what happened. (Asides are mine.)

> But Jesus immediately said to them: "Take courage! It is I. Don't be afraid."
>
> "Lord, if it's you," Peter replied, "tell me to come to you on the water." (He was on his diving board, ready to jump in.)
>
> "Come," he said. (No turning back, Peter. You have direct confirmation from the Lord. What's your next step?)
>
> Then Peter got down out of the boat, walked on

the water and came toward Jesus. (And there we have it. He launched into thin air, my friend. The step that put it all into motion had been accomplished.) But when he saw the wind, he was afraid and, beginning to sink, cried out, "Lord, save me!" (Wait a minute, that's not how the story is supposed to go. We prepare, we act, then everything turns out just right. Right? Not so much, apparently. Something is missing.)

Immediately Jesus reached out His hand and caught him. "You of little faith," he said, "why did you doubt?" (Ah, there's our missing ingredient. Faith. Courage must be directly linked with faith, or we sink. Good to know.)

And when they climbed into the boat, the wind died down. Then those who were in the boat wor-shiped him, saying, "Truly you are the Son of God." (I wouldn't be surprised if Peter was too busy having a minor heart attack to worship at the moment. There's a point in faith when we experience something amaz-ing and Jesus shows up and proves that He's every-thing He's promised to be, and it's almost too much for us to take in. I wonder if Peter had trouble talking for the rest of the day.)

And so we come to you, my friend. What's that step that will kick everything into gear? Have you married your courage to your faith, or is one of them still lacking? It might help to remem-ber that Jesus was right next to Peter the whole time; He didn't let him sink too far. Gather your courage and do it!

Refocus, Refocus!

There are times when we follow God and the challenges in front of us frighten the socks right off our feet. It happens to the best of us; remember that Peter started to sink even when Jesus was right there with him! But we can learn from Peter's example. We can refuse to be distracted by the waves and the immensity of the task. God loves us, He protects us, and He will not fail us.

Our fear will flee when we focus on Jesus instead of the problem.

STUDY QUESTIONS

1. Rate your fear of God's request on a scale of 1 to 10. A 1 means you aren't nervous at all, and a 10 means you're possibly about to throw up out of sheer terror.

2. Let's get it out in the open—what is the worst possible thing that could happen to you or your family if you obey? What do you think God is going to do about that possibility?

3. Are you focused on your fear or God's provision and power? What can you do to focus more completely on God's power?

4. Study the following Scriptures about God's power. Write down the ones that calm your fears.

   a. Exodus 14:10–18
   b. Psalm 107:13–16
   c. Acts 5:38–39
   d. Hebrews 12:18–29

The goal of faithfulness is not that we will do work for God, but that He will be free to do His work through us. God calls us to His service and places tremendous responsibilities on us. He expects no complaining on our part and offers no explanation on His part. God wants to use us as He used His own Son.

Oswald Chambers, *My Utmost for His Highest*

Heather and Her Family Move to Alaska

Heather and her husband, Rich, didn't get married with the intention of becoming missionaries to anyplace, let alone to Alaska. They were living their normal lives with two children in southwest Michigan, interested in ministry but without a specific idea of what God wanted them to do. Conversations with their pastor sparked the idea of an Alaskan mission field. I called Heather on the phone, 3,500 miles away, and we had a nice chat. Do you know that calling Alaska sounds just as clear as calling the next town? Technology is amazing, I tell you. Here is what she shared:

After a short-term missions trip to the region to feel out the possibilities, Rich and I returned home committed to following God's call to Alaska. However, the road to the north was not so smooth. Fundraising was a struggle from the beginning, and the actual move to Alaska was derailed after several years of work and planning when we realized the ministry we had hoped to join was not a good fit.

We were stumped. Had God closed a door? What were we supposed to do next? We started praying for God's will, no matter the outcome. And we told God we were fine with going and fine with staying. We tried to be flexible, and we tried to move ahead through the indecision.

After almost two years of preparing, I made contact with a completely new ministry. Alaska Youth for Christ has a ministry for teenagers in jail and those recently released from the system. The juvenile justice ministry needed new workers, and my qualifications were a good fit. The money we had already raised was transferred to the new ministry and our family was off! Alaska-bound!

As soon as we got to Alaska, everything was smooth and perfect, right?

No. Incorrect.

Our family has struggled through all sorts of problems while ministering. We had hoped to keep our home in Michigan and rent it out, but being landlords from more than 3,500 miles away proved impossible. Then my parents both became very, very sick, and my mom died. We were needed in Michigan, and we were needed in Alaska.

It wasn't just problems from back home either. Our time in Alaska had its own set of challenges. I developed health problems. Finances are difficult because the cost of living in Anchorage is high, and the economy slowdown made things even worse. Health care costs for our family have skyrocketed. Ministry work itself is a challenge because kids in jail do not just suddenly decide to make good decisions because the chaplain stops by and chats.

We stay encouraged by celebrating the little victories when they come. Sometimes a girl in the system will decide to keep her baby instead of having an abortion. I celebrate. Sometimes a kid will call for good advice. That makes me feel great.

And I plan for the future. Working with these kids has shown me a void in Anchorage—affordable housing for kids who are newly out on their own. The young adults frequently end up at the homeless shelter, where they are often lured into sex trafficking and drugs. I'd love to run a faith-based home for them where they can afford to pay the low rent, live with people who care, and learn the life skills they need.

I take this from Heather and Rich's example: We must keep our focus on where God wants us. We can't get derailed by problems, fears, or frustrations. Even when it feels like we face more losses than wins, when our eyes are on His direction, His plan, and His provision—we are successful. ■

CHAPTER 14

Continuing Faithfully

GALATIANS 6:7-9

Do not be deceived. God cannot be mocked. A man reaps what he sows. Whoever sows to please their flesh, from the flesh will reap destruction; whoever sows to please the Spirit, from the Spirit will reap eternal life. Let us not become weary in doing good, for at the proper time we will reap a harvest if we do not give up.

The last chapter focused on sucking it up and marching forward, even when the panic sets in and we need every bit of courage we can find. This chapter talks about what happens after the panic, after the courage—when we realize we're in this for the long haul and it's tedious.

Imagine a bride. She's dressed in an outrageously expensive gown. Her father waits at her side. Her hands hold a bouquet of beautiful flowers. The church is decorated, and everyone she knows watches as she walks down the aisle. Her groom stands near the altar, right next to the preacher. She suddenly realizes that she's about to legally and publicly bind herself to a man who may or may not turn out to be a decent husband. Is she looking at fifty years of companionship and fun, or five years of agony before a screaming divorce? She panics. The world goes woozy, and she clutches at her father's arm so she doesn't faint. Deep breath in, deep breath out. She gathers her courage and walks to the front. What is life without stepping out into faith?

Fast-forward seven years. The honeymoon is over; the bloom is off the rose. The bride and groom are each twenty pounds heavier. The mortgage is about $30,000 more than they can comfortably afford, so he works overtime every night. The three children are sick with colds, and our former bride is two months late and feeling nauseous. Her mother-in-law just announced she is selling her house and moving into the spare bedroom.

The wife fantasizes of escaping to the tropics where she will become a server in a beach resort. She will serve delicious icy beverages to tanned and handsome people all day, and her only responsibility will be to wipe down the counter. Ah, paradise. However, reality being what it is, she knows that the husband, mortgage, children, pregnancy, and mother-in-law will all follow her to the resort, and that is going to be a tight squeeze.

Real life, my friend, is not paradise. Real life is often tedious. It requires step after step after step, until you can look back and realize how far you've come. But the journey is often long, strenuous, and *boring*. It's still God's will, though. We need to journey onward until God tells us we've arrived at our destination. The way to God's plan is rarely instantaneous. Every once in a while God does a miracle quickly, and we love to hear those stories. Sadly, that's not usually the way it works.

Speaking of long, drawn out, tedious journeys, let's discuss the Israelites wandering in the desert for forty years. *Forty years*. That is enough to try the patience of any saint. Forty years in the desert. No permanent house. No permanent neighborhood. No permanent bathrooms, schoolhouses, or shopping malls. It would literally be the worst camping trip *ever*.

Before we begin, I need to clarify one possible large difference between the Israelites' trip through the desert and your life: the Jews wandered because they had rebelled, and God was not happy with them. This may not be the case with your life. You may be obeying to the best of your ability, but God may still be taking you on the slow boat to China. I do not know why He is doing this, but it's nothing new. Don't panic or take it personally. Instead, take this time to grow closer to God while you wait. Spend daily time in prayer and Bible reading. Learn a new hobby. Clean out the fridge. Something!

Anyway, let's move back to the Israelites and their long, drawn-out journey. Numbers 33 outlines their entire trip. I won't rewrite it here, as it's long and tedious—just like the trip. At any given time they could have given up. They could have settled in a spot with water and pastureland. They could have found a large city and joined the inhabitants. They could have split up and gone their separate ways. What would have happened to God's people if they had not completed the journey?

It would not have ended the way God had wanted it to, that's for sure. The only way to complete God's plan was step after step for forty years *until He said they were done.* Forty years of setting up camp, digging new latrines, and rearranging the neighborhood. It was only by the process of slowly but surely following God's will that they finally arrived in the Promised Land. Don't give up hope if you find yourself on the most boring journey of your life. Keep going, and God will eventually lead you to your destination.

Different Plants Have Different Seasons of Harvest

Who loves to garden? I do, I do! One of the blessings and curses of gardening is that every plant has a different season of harvest or bloom. The tulip tree blossoms every spring, but tomatoes are ready in the late summer until the first frost. Keeping track of each plant for optimum production or beauty can be hard.

Two years ago, I had an onion in my pantry that sprouted. (My produce management system is lax, I admit.) I was in the middle of planting a bunch of stuff in the front flower bed, so I trooped outside and planted the bulb right next to the hollyhocks. It was actually quite an interesting addition to the garden. It grew a stalk about two feet tall with a round flowery thing on the top. If you touched it, it scented the air like onion. Since onions are cheap, I didn't try to harvest it; I just left it there for entertainment's sake. A year later it grew back. Finally, this fall I pulled it out because it was starting to look gnarly. At the root end, there was a new huge onion. (Or was it the same onion, refreshed and matured? I'm not sure.) Apparently onions can take a long time to grow! Who knew? It only takes mold about three weeks to grow on my leftover green beans in the fridge. (Perhaps too much information?) Everything runs on its own schedule of maturity.

Galatians 6:9 speaks to this very issue: "Let us not become weary in doing good, for at the proper time we will reap a harvest if we do not give up." Diligent farmers know that they can't just give up and let everything take care of itself. The barn will fall down. The weeds will overtake the crops. Someone needs to get out in the field and bring in the harvest or it will rot. Diligence and wisdom lead to a productive yield, just as diligence and wisdom lead to completing God's plan to His satisfaction.

That passage in Galatians is key; let's look at all of it to get a more complete picture.

> Do not be deceived: God cannot be mocked. A man reaps what he sows. Whoever sows to please their flesh, from the flesh will reap destruction; whoever sows to please the Spirit, from the Spirit will reap eternal life. Let us not become weary in doing good, for at the proper time we will reap a harvest if we do not give up. Therefore, as we have opportunity, let us do good to all people, especially to those who belong to the family of believers. (6:7–10)

This passage teaches us that there's more to the journey with God than just plodding along, day after dusty day. If we sow good seeds (of worship, loving others, kindness, faithfulness, obedience), then our harvest will bear the fruit that comes from that effort. Of course our *salvation* doesn't come through our own efforts, but the life we live in Christ can be pitiful or abundant— it only depends on what we're sowing. We have no control over the length of time between planting and harvest. That's not for us to decide! But what we sow and how we tend our lives is up to us; the thousands of daily choices we make determine how bountiful our harvest will be when the time comes. Are we willing to do this well?

We could make many, many applications from this passage, but we don't have many, many pages to go into them all. But I would like to pull out one more point. Did you notice that mention of the Holy Spirit? It says that if we sow to please Him, then we will reap eternal life. Jesus' ministry on earth was actually pretty short, especially if we compare His time to that of Moses or King David. He had three years to teach and train a bunch of random men. But when He left, He made sure that the Holy Spirit would come to help them on their daily journey. Those fishermen went on to become empowered apostles! Their harvests were more than abundant; we're still seeing the fruit of their labor two thousand years later.

The same Holy Spirit that Jesus sent to His disciples is here with us today. He is ready to help us along the journey, and He wants the harvest to be plentiful. He is the secret to success when we need to continue faithfully. Have we tuned our ears to hear Him and our hearts to seek Him? Do we even know how to do that? I know we often don't do it well. I run about all by myself and completely forget that the Holy Spirit has anything to add to my efforts. But I do know this—when I remember that He's there and is far more capable than I am, I ask Him for help. A simple cry of "Holy Spirit, please work in my heart!" saves the day. He comes. He gives strength for a journey that is far too long for me and helps me reap a harvest I never could have sown alone.

He can do the same for you, if you are willing to ask. If you're a few years or decades into a project God started for you, don't give up! I know it can seem like the harvest is never going to happen. Take heart that the project may be one of those forty-years-in-the-desert deals, not a teleporter-through-the-decades deals. Beam me up, Scotty! (Good luck with that. I've been trying for years, and apparently God does not watch old *Star Trek* episodes.)

Perhaps you are at the exciting beginning of your journey with God, when all the adrenaline is charging. You have no idea what this whole chapter is about—yet. I hope you'll remember these thoughts when you need them. When the journey grows long and boring, when the harvest appears too far off—remember these words. Look to the Holy Spirit to give you the strength to continue. And have faith that an end will one day come!

But Is It Really Supposed to Take This Long?

Perhaps you have been waiting forty years for God's will to come to fruition, and it's still not long enough. The initial panic changed to tedium, and after years of tedium and waiting, you only have hopelessness. You realize that the dream you had, the understanding you had, is never going to exist in the way you expected it. Your bright dream has dimmed to a tiny flicker: "Why am I bothering with all this sacrifice?" "Why do I still pray for him?" "Has God changed His mind?"

Hebrews 11 is titled "By Faith" in my NIV Bible. It begins with this: "Now faith is confidence in what we hope for and assurance about what we do not see." It continues with a huge list of the biblical giants who did great things for God but never saw the end result. In fact, if we step back and take a wide-angle view, we are *still* waiting for the end result. Each time we obey God we are adding another brushstroke to the giant painting of history. In the end, the picture will show every part of history from creation to eternity. But now we can only wait in faith for the painting to be completed.

Take a few moments to read Hebrews 11. If you don't have your Bible handy, I'll summarize it for you:

- ▶ By faith we believe that God created the world out of nothing.
- ▶ Abel offered God a better sacrifice by faith (the NIV study note says perhaps Cain offered God a sacrifice as a formality, without faith being involved).
- ▶ Enoch was taken from this life without death because he pleased God, and pleasing God requires faith.
- ▶ Noah built an ark on faith because he was working with circumstances that no one had ever experienced.
- ▶ Abraham left for a new home using only faith as a map because he did not know where he was going.
- ▶ Abraham and Sarah became parents because they had faith that God could enable them, even though their bodies were completely unable.
- ▶ Abraham was willing to offer Isaac as a sacrifice because he had faith that God could raise him from the dead. He obeyed even to the point of his own child's life!
- ▶ By faith Isaac blessed Jacob's and Esau's futures.
- ▶ Joseph worshiped as he leaned on his staff, just as he was about to die.
- ▶ Joseph spoke in faith, knowing that the Israelites would eventually leave Egypt.
- ▶ Moses' parents hid him in faith, understanding that there was something extraordinary going on.

▶ Because he had faith, Moses chose a hard life of leadership over an easy life as the princess's son.

▶ The Israelites passed through the Red Sea by faith.

▶ The walls of Jericho fell because of faith.

▶ Rahab the prostitute was saved because of her faith.

This list doesn't even get to the others who acted according
to faith—clinging to hope in the face of terror, difficulty, and
discomfort.

The chapter ends with these verses: "These were all com-
mended for their faith, yet none of them received what had been
promised, since God had planned something better for us so that
only together with us would they be made perfect" (Hebrews
11:39–40). This is just another way of saying we're all waiting for
the painting to be finished one day in the future.

I am not denying that waiting in faith is hard. When results
are absent, it seems like the work and sacrifice involved are in
vain. But for those of us sitting here in the twenty-first century,
we look back on the people from Hebrews 11 and think *"Holy
cats! These people were brave! They did the impossible because God
was asking them to work for Him. And look at the results!"* I don't
know about you, but I would hardly consider any of their sacrifices to be in vain.

This is something to remember when our own sowing, weed-
ing, and pruning appear to be endless, bearing no fruit. When the
results just aren't there, step back and realize that the harvest is
not yet ready.

What If the End Is Not Near?

Modern life has cheated us. It's given us unrealistic expectations
about how fast everything should be completed. We put a bag
of popcorn in the microwave, and in less than three minutes we

have fluffy, buttery, salty deliciousness. We don't have to go to the field in May to sow the seeds, weed the soil for months, chase off the wildlife with bows and arrows, and finally harvest the corn in the fall. We just go to the store, swipe our magic card, and put a lumpy bag in the presto-chango box. Popcorn time!

Our food supply isn't the only thing on warp speed. Thanks to acrylic nails, hair extensions, and plastic surgery I could look like a beauty pageant queen by Friday afternoon, given enough money and an opening in the beauty team's schedule. *I don't even have to wait to grow my own hair.* How ludicrous is that? In comparison, God's plans can feel stalled out when the real problem is our unrealistic expectations.

My point is this: We may never get to see the end result of God's plan. We have no way of knowing how long it will take, because He doesn't work in microwave popcorn time. The end may be years beyond us. We may be a step in the middle of the plan, and generations beyond us may be counting on us to do our part now. Keep going! Have faith that God will take care of what is beyond your line of vision.

My dad is an original farm boy, Vietnam veteran wild child. I don't know half of the stories from his youth, and I probably never will. While he did spend some time in church as a young boy, by the time he went off to Vietnam, his Sunday school attendance had grown lax. Let's just say that if he had continued down his original path, I might have been raised on the farm running moonshine and growing Mary Jane on the back forty.

But back in the early 1980s my dad was working with a Christian man named Steve. Steve and Dad became friends, and our family's history was rewritten. My parents started going to church regularly, and we three children were raised to know and respect God. Our family is far from perfect, but think of how different it could have been! I teach Sunday school and (apparently) write books to encourage people to follow God. This is far more satisfying than running moonshine and growing pot. I think. I mean, I'm assuming this is true. It's far less stressful, I know that for sure.

I haven't seen Steve in more than twenty years. He might not have any idea of how his obedience to God has affected my life, my children's lives, and the lives of the kids in my Sunday school class. Now, even *your* life has been affected, because this book is a result of when he was brave enough to befriend my dad and encourage him in Christ.

When we step out and obey God, the ripple effect continues far beyond our own limited perspective and years on this earth. Nothing we do for God is insignificant. He will bless and multiply our efforts. By faith we believe in what we cannot see!

STUDY QUESTIONS

1. Do you have a dream or a project from God that is taking a really long time to show fruit?
   a. If so, how long have you waited?
   b. What emotions are you feeling now? How often do you want to quit or give up hope?

2. Hebrews 11 lists multiple people who trusted God and acted completely in faith.
   a. Which person speaks to you the loudest? Why?
   b. What aspects of his or her life could you develop?
   c. How do you think this person handled the times of fear and lack of faith?

3. When you think about the world's history as a huge, unfinished painting . . .
   a. How do you fit into the big picture?
   b. What changes do you think you have brought to the world?
   c. What effect would you like to have on the future?

4. Please look up the following Bible passages and consider how long these people waited for God to make good on his promise:

   a. Genesis 12:1–4 and 21:1–5

   b. 1 Samuel 16:11–13 and 2 Samuel 2:1–4 (all those chapters between these two passages are stories of David waiting to ascend to the throne)

   c. Luke 2:21–38

   d. Acts 1:10–11; Revelation 22:7, 20

> Jesus compared the Kingdom of God to the inexplicable bounty reaped by the man who throws seed on the land. With that simple act, the farmer's work is done. He hibernates for the winter, sleeps late, goes bowling, watches television, washes clothes, repairs the hole in the roof, and travels to Delaware, New Mexico, and Oregon to visit his three children. Whether it is night or day, whether the farmer is asleep or awake, at home or on the road, the seed he scattered sprouts and grows. He does not have a clue how it happened. The earth does it all without his help. First the shoot, then the ear, then the full grain in the ear. One sunlit morning, he has six buttermilk pancakes and four slices of Canadian bacon for breakfast, walks out the door, scratches his head at the ripened grain, and reaps his harvest (Mark 4:26–29).
>
> **Brennan Manning,** *Ruthless Trust*

My Profound Hope

It is my profound hope that by now you're filled with one simple thought:

God and I can do this together. We really can.

))) **You and God can do this together. You really can.**

We've dissected stories from the Bible. We've been filled with Jesus' words. We've learned about our place in God's eternal plan and our place in relationship to others. I've told you many ridiculous stories about my own faith journey and bolstered you with stories from my friends. But I do have one little story from the Old Testament that I'd like to retell in my own words before we part ways, because I need to tootle off to write more books and you need to do whatever it is that God has called you to do. If you don't understand why I put this story in the conclusion, then I have failed to write anything useful. I hope it will make perfect sense.

Hey Gideon, Why Are You Hiding in That Winepress?

In Judges 6 and 7, Israel had once again done evil in God's eyes, so He took His protection away from them. As a result, the Midianites and other people groups were ravaging all the Israelites' fields, livestock, and livelihood. It had gotten so bad that the Jews had started hiding in the mountains. You know it's bad when you have to start hiding in the mountains.

The Israelites humbled themselves before God once again, and He sent a prophet to tell them, "I saved you from Egyptian slavery. I drove out your enemies and gave you their land. Then I told you I was your God and you weren't supposed to worship other gods. But you have not listened to me!" The Bible does not record God adding, "You stubborn, ignorant goats" to the end of that lecture, but I know I would have.

He may have been upset with them, but apparently His heart was softened by their cries for mercy. The angel of the Lord went to see Gideon, who was threshing his wheat in a winepress so the enemies would not see it, steal his food, and destroy the whole farm. The angel said to Gideon, "The LORD is with you, mighty warrior."

What follows is a "Jessie paraphrase" of the story:

Gideon replied, "No, I think you may be mistaken. If God is with us, why am I forced to hide my grain in a winepress? God has abandoned us."

The Lord said to him, "Go, in the strength you have. . . . Am I not sending you?"

"But, Lord," Gideon replied, "I don't think you understand the full situation here. I'm the peon in my clan, and frankly, my clan isn't all that hot. We're not important or strong or leadership oriented."

The Lord answered, "I will be with you, and you're going to smite all the Midianites."

Gideon replied, "If you still think I'm the one, can you wait here while I go get a sacrifice ready?"

God said He would wait.

Gideon took the resources he had and brought an offering to the Lord. The angel said to take the sacrifice and put it on a rock. Gideon obeyed, even though it was getting really weird. The angel touched the sacrifice and everything blew into a big fireball. Then the angel disappeared. When Gideon realized he had just been face-to-face with the angel of the Lord, he nearly had a heart attack. God told him to calm down; he wasn't going to die. Gideon was so amazed that he built an altar to the Lord right there.

The same night God told him to kill one of his father's bulls, take down an altar to Baal, build a new altar for the Lord, and sacrifice the bull on it. Now, dealing with the angel of the Lord near the winepress was one thing, but this was going to catch him grief from everyone in the family. Since Gideon was kind of a chicken, he took ten of his servants and obeyed God—at night.

Just as he had suspected, no one was super excited about the new altar in the morning. In fact, the men of the town told Gideon's father that Gideon needed to die because of his gall. Joash (Gideon's father) pointed out to the angry mob that if Baal was really a god he could take care of himself. Lucky for Gideon this worked, and they didn't kill him.

While all this was going on in Israel, the enemies were gathering. (If this were a movie, the music would be getting creepy and ominous.) The Spirit of the Lord came upon Gideon, and he rose up to be the leader that God needed him to be. He called all the people to join him, and they did just that.

But first Gideon needed to make certain that he was doing the right thing. He asked God to do two miracles on two different nights. One night he wanted the grass dry and the fleece wet. The next night he wanted the opposite (not a man of great imagination, apparently). He must have been satisfied, because chapter 7 starts with Gideon camping with all his men at the spring of Harod.

God said to Gideon, in effect, "Nope. Too many men. We need

to get rid of some of them. I don't want this looking like it was accomplished because the army was strong. If anyone is scared, send him home." Twenty-two thousand men left. Ten thousand stayed.

God responded: "We still have too many men. Let's go get a drink of water, and I'll sort them out for you." Gideon obeyed, and God wanted only three hundred men to stay. The three hundred who stayed took over the provisions and trumpets of the ones who left. Poor Gideon was probably hoping that he'd just get speared to death to get it over with, but God gave him a final nudge of encouragement. "Go down to the enemy camp and listen. You'll be encouraged to attack," God promised.

Gideon did just that, and he heard an enemy talking about how he had a nutty dream about a loaf of bread crushing a tent. His friend (enemy No. 2) responded, "Well, that's it. We're all going to die because God has given us into Gideon's hands." Gideon was so encouraged by the dream's interpretation that he worshiped God and returned to camp.

He divided the three hundred men into three groups and armed them with . . . clay pots with candles inside and with trumpets. That's it. Who needs a spear or a slingshot or a set of flaming arrows? Not Gideon, and not God.

Gideon had finally grown out of his scared-weeny stage, and he said to his men, "Watch me and follow my lead. When we get to the camp, do what I do. Blow your trumpets and shout, 'For the Lord and for Gideon!'"

They reached the camp just after the changing of the guard, at the beginning of the middle watch. They blew their trumpets, broke their jars, and shouted, "A sword for the Lord and for Gideon!" Each man stood in his place while the Midianites started running and attacking one another. The Israelites who had left soon joined back in, and victory was theirs.

I'll summarize a wee bit here so we're clear before we leave each other's company:

- ▶ The Israelites had sinned, but repented. God saw their humble hearts.
- ▶ Gideon was scared and running low on testosterone, but he chose an attitude of obedience.
- ▶ He listened carefully and made sure he really understood what God needed him to do.
- ▶ Gideon followed His instructions exactly and did it in God's perfect timing.
- ▶ He offered a sacrifice, which certainly cost him something.
- ▶ Gideon's friends and family were none too pleased with his obedience, but he obeyed God anyway.
- ▶ He sacrificed his own comfort by stepping past his fear and perception of himself.
- ▶ His plan was not God's plan. He ended up with a tiny percentage of the original army, but he was flexible.
- ▶ He picked his army carefully by following God's directions.
- ▶ He sucked up the tiny amount of courage he had lurking in his chest and stepped out with God. He kept going even when the enemy outnumbered his army by a ridiculous amount. He did not give up when all he had was three hundred men armed with pottery.
- ▶ God accomplished His will. Gideon's obedience was the catalyst for that amazing story, but the glory must go completely to God.

If God can use Gideon, He can use me. And He can certainly use you. Be strong and courageous! Be strong and courageous! Be strong and courageous . . .

STUDY QUESTIONS

1. Are you feeling better about this assignment God is asking you to complete?

2. Are you strong enough to complete this on your own?

3. What amazing things do you think God will do as you obey Him?

4. What material possessions, resources, or relationships are you willing to offer as a sacrifice to accomplish your part of this project?

5. Who will receive the glory for this?

6. In conclusion, here are some verses to help us focus on God, who is strong enough to complete any project He initiates!

   a. 2 Chronicles 6:14–15
   b. Psalm 9:1–10
   c. Psalm 27:1–6
   d. Romans 8:28, 37–39
   e. Colossians 1:15–23
   f. 2 Thessalonians 1:11–12
   g. 2 Thessalonians 2:13–17

Afterword

A few days after I finished the rough draft of this manuscript, I called to Eric from our room. "Hey," I said. "Did you hear the church on Oakland Drive has a job opening for a secretary?"

And for the first time in two years, Eric *didn't* say, "You don't need a job."

He said, "That might work."

Stunned to hear him agree, I applied that night. A few weeks later, I finished all my manuscript editing for real and hit the magic button to send my final efforts to Miranda, my delightful editor. Two hours later, a call came through from the church with a job offer. I don't find this timing to be a coincidence.

So now every morning I scoot into my little office and make copies and write bulletins and other such things. I've been given a whole new opportunity to be flexible, to wait for God's timing, and to see His provision as I balance family, work, and new writing projects. I'm reminded daily that our lives are a fluid river, moving where God takes us next. We were never meant to be stagnant pools. We were never meant to cower on the couch with our ears plugged, pretending we can't hear God when He calls.

I can't wait to hear all your stories about where God's taking *you* next. Please, look me up and tell me all about it:

- Blog: jessieclemence.com
- Facebook: JessieClemence
- Twitter: @JessieClemence4

I hope to hear from you soon!

Notes

Chapter 3

1. Sophie Hudson, *A Little Salty to Cut the Sweet: Southern Stories of Faith, Family, and Fifteen Pounds of Bacon* (Carol Stream, IL: Tyndale, 2013), p. 106.
2. Jason Sleight, personal email, June 2013.

Chapter 4

1. Priscilla Shirer, *He Speaks to Me: Preparing to Hear from God* (Chicago: Moody, 2006), p. 26.

Chapter 6

1. FinAid: The Smart Student Guide to Financial Aid, accessed February 12, 2014, http://www.finaid.org/calculators/loan payments.phtml.

Chapter 7

1. Lysa TerKeurst, *Unglued: Making Wise Choices in the Midst of Raw Emotions* (Grand Rapids: Zondervan, 2012), p. 135.

I'd Like to Take a Minute to Thank a Few People

First, to my blogging friends who contributed to this book with their own stories (take a minute and check out their blogs! You'll be glad you did):

- David Welford at nwelford.wordpress.com
- Cheri Swalwell at journeysfromtheheartofawifeand mother.wordpress.com
- Anthony Baker at therecoveringlegalist.com
- Cheri Fields at creationscience4kids.com

And now, no less important but slightly less bloggy:

- Betsy in Texas
- Maggie and Dewayne in Central Asia
- Heather in Alaska

And now, closer to home:

- Jason Sleight, pastor of West Kalamazoo Christian Church. I'm sorry I keep yelling things at you from the back row while you preach. Thanks so much for all your help with this book. We truly appreciate everything you and the leadership do for our congregation.
- Miranda Gardner, who has supported this project from the very beginning. I owe you a kidney or other organ of your choice. Let me know if you ever need one.
- Audrey and Caleb, who endured a whole lot of snow days while Mom was locked up inside her bedroom and kept yelling things like, "Be quiet! I'm trying to

write a book!" from the other side of the door. I love you so much!

- Eric, who is the sole human reason I haven't quit writing. Thanks for your endless encouragement and willingness to share money with me so I don't starve to death. You are the best.

- And, of course, to the Author and Finisher of our faith: You wrote it first; thanks for including me in this tiny part of the journey.